The Double-Purpose High School

EDGAR STARR BARNEY PROJECT
of the HEBREW TECHNICAL INSTITUTE
36 Stuyvesant Street, New York 3, N. Y.

THE EDGAR STARR BARNEY PROJECT is the research and service department of the Hebrew Technical Institute. Founded in 1884, the Institute was the first free vocational school established in New York City for 14- to 17-year-old boys. It was supported entirely by voluntary contributions. When the present system of public vocational schools was well established, the HTI was discontinued as a school (1939), but it remains active as an endowed nonsectarian organization, concerned with problems of technical and vocational education throughout the country. Edgar Starr Barney was the distinguished principal of the school until his death in 1938.

In 1948, *Education for an Industrial Age,* by Alfred Kahler and Ernest Hamburger, published by Cornell University Press, was sponsored by the Edgar Starr Barney Project.

This book is the first of a new series planned by the Project.

The Double-Purpose High School

Closing the Gap Between Vocational and Academic Preparation

by FRANKLIN J. KELLER

Principal, *Metropolitan Vocational High School*
Technical Director, *Edgar Starr Barney Project*
New York City

 HARPER & BROTHERS, *Publishers, New York*

Library of Congress catalog card number: 53-8541

Contents

Acknowledgments

In order that the findings of this study might attain as high a degree of validity as possible, outstanding educators were appointed as an Advisory Committee. They have given generously from their store of knowledge and experience:

Edward Berman, Assistant Superintendent of Schools and Director of Vocational Education, Bayonne, N. J.

Lynn A. Emerson, Professor of Industrial Education, Cornell University.

Marcella R. Lawler, Associate Professor of Education, Teachers College, Columbia University.

J. Wayne Wrightstone, Director of Educational Research, Board of Education, New York City.

Thanks for valuable services are also extended to Nathan Luloff, Technical Assistant of the study; to Irving Metz, Executive Secretary, Hebrew Technical Institute; and to Raymond G. Fuller, who aided in editorial tasks.

Preface

This book is compounded of facts, experience, and conviction.

The facts point to an inevitable conclusion: one + one = ONE. It means that if you add academic preparation to vocational preparation you have EDUCATION, in large letters—bigger, better, functioning, interesting, and pleasant to take.

Experience with young people—experience of the principals who have contributed these facts, along with their own opinions —indicates that enough young minds are avid for this kind of education to make it a cause of tremendous impact.

The conviction of the author and consultants is that this is an area in education that needs loving cultivation; that it provides the interest, the "doing," the intellectual stimulation calculated to discover and develop the whole person. While we adults have put the words down on paper, the book has really been written by the young people about whom it is concerned. In the chapter entitled "Who Are These Boys and Girls?" even the *words* are theirs.

So, we wrote this book to bolster the convictions of the like-minded and to change the minds of the others. We wrote it for those who control the destinies of the young. First of all, for parents as parents, and then for parents (and nonparents) as community leaders, as members of boards of education, as superintendents, as principals, as teachers. We wrote for the current ruling generation who are making the world and are preparing the younger generation in the high schools to live in it. Our conviction is that those high schools must be the best that the mind of man can contrive. For these young people are all right.

April 1, 1953   FRANKLIN J. KELLER

The Double-Purpose
High School

I. You Are a Parent—a Schoolman—a Citizen

What kinds of schools do you want for your children?

You are a parent. Your son is bent upon being a machinist or on going to sea. Your daughter wants passionately to be a dress designer or a nurse. Along with intense interest, these children have talent in their chosen fields. They also have the intelligence necessary for success in the liberal arts. In fact, you want them to go to college to become, as so many parents say, "really educated." But both boy and girl are interested in *doing* the things they want to learn, and they want to do them *now*. Books leave them mildly warm, but machinery and tools and laboratories and activity really excite them. They will learn their trades because of their compelling interests.

So you ask: How can I feed their interest through useful occupations, and at the same time prepare them for higher education? And will they be interested in and benefit from college when they get there? This book gives you the answer. They can learn trades and prepare for college in a number of "double-purpose" high schools in the United States.

You are the principal of a high school—academic or vocational. You have in your school the children of the parent of whom we have just spoken. Can you organize your school to prepare the same young people to enter both trades and college? Our study of high schools in the United States shows that you can definitely do so. We give in some detail the stories of a dozen "double-purpose" schools.

1

You are a superintendent of schools or member of a board of education. Can you organize a school system that will provide the same young people with occupational competence and a liberal education? We say, yes, you can.

You should carefully note that this double-purpose school is for boys and girls who have a deep interest in a useful occupation and a receptiveness for the liberal arts. They may comprise as many as 10 per cent of the total high school population. Therefore, in this book we are not describing the "comprehensive high school," which, by definition, provides for *all* the boys and girls in a community. The present double-purpose school is a kind of trial run for the complete task of the American High School, which is now being studied by the Edgar Starr Barney Project.

Like any other serious book, this one should strengthen the beliefs of some people and may shatter those of others. It should make them do the things they believe in. Not only must it command the interest of the "general public," but it must gain the approval of "professionals"—educators, school administrators, teachers. Not only must it stimulate the general public (the people who own the schools and whose children attend them), but it must enlist the understanding and militant action of the schoolmen.

It would be fine to make this solely a general interest book, but unless it captures the imagination and enlightens the understanding of the educator, nothing will happen in the schools. The educator wants to see the research data. For him the book has to be a "technical study." For John Q. Public it should be a practical interpretation of his child's desires.

So, this study of double-purpose schools has itself a double purpose. One is to convince the lay parent of the effectiveness of bridging the academic-vocational gap, and the second is to demonstrate to the educator the technique of organizing a double-purpose school.

This book is about education for free youth. It is about education, not just about training for jobs, certainly not about vocational education as something apart or different from *education*, or as a special, subsidiary branch. Education for free youth must be education for *all* youth, with a good deal of common content but with a considerable degree of specialization to provide for difference in capacity and interest. This has to be recognized not only in theory but in practical school curricula.

Free youth, of course, are youth who are free to learn, free to do, free to speak, whatever they *can* learn, do, and speak. They are youth in a democracy. They have freedom of opportunity and choice, educational and vocational. They can choose the kind of education they want. The community should not penalize them by the confining narrowness or the vague broadness of its educational offering. They should enjoy both a broad cultural heritage and a highly specialized occupational training.

Some seventy years ago the term "vocational education" was little known and less practiced in American secondary schools. Yet today, of the approximately 24,500 public high schools in the United States, almost half offer some kind of hand, machine, or laboratory work. True, much of it is not vocational education, not even good general education, but it is a recognition of the growing importance of occupational training and "learning by doing" as educational forces. Paradoxically, this new element in American education is one of the oldest forms of education. What has changed in the past seven decades—and what we would hope to see change even more—is the concept of vocational education as something more than mere training for a craft or job.

This book is the result of a widespread cooperative study. It was originally sent for criticism to five hundred vocational and general educators—commissioners, superintendents, directors, teachers—as well as to laymen interested in education. Almost exactly one hundred responses came back. They have ranged from complete and enthusiastic approval to fundamental differences in philosophy. All have been kindly and generous.

To these critics and coauthors we are deeply grateful. We use the word "critic" in the sense of its first and most honorable definition: One who expresses a seasoned opinion on any matter as a work of art or a course of conduct, involving a judgment of its value, truth or righteousness, an appreciation of its beauty or technique, or an interpretation. We have weighed all the comments carefully and have either written them into the manuscript or acknowledged them as tenable points of view. Some of them relate to issues so basic or generalized, or both, that we comment upon them specifically in Chapters II and IX.

To recapitulate: this book is designed for all who play any part in the planning, organization, and maintenance of schools—especially secondary schools. Once the elementary school was the common school. Today the high school has become the common school and probably the most controversial field of public education. Writing for a large and diverse audience always incurs the danger of spreading the subject matter thin and confusing the issues. We have taken pains to throw a spotlight on one phase of secondary education and to explore its potentialities.

Essentially, this phase concerns such organization of secondary schools as to prepare young people at one and the same time for a suitable occupation and for entrance to college, especially a college that will continue the preparation for both occupation and culture. This brief statement deserves considerable elaboration and some qualification. In the main body of the book the continued implication for people is that "expert knowledge," in the words of Alfred North Whitehead, "will give them the ground to start from and their culture will lead them as deep as philosophy and as high as art." "Expert knowledge" may be taken here to mean "vocational education."

This volume answers the question: Can young people with aptitudes for doing and intellect for knowing, while in high school, prepare for admission to both occupation and college? This question concerns all those now preparing for college who wish to learn a trade, or are learning a trade and may wish to enter college. The group constitutes a small percentage of the total high school population—perhaps 10 per cent—but an important percentage. Therefore, this research deals with only part of the whole secondary school program and is a forerunner to our study: How much and what kind of vocational education at what age?—the problem of the comprehensive high school.

II. The Basic Problem

Closing the vocational-academic gap

"Culture is activity of thought, and receptiveness to beauty and humane feelings. Scraps of information have nothing to do with it. A merely well-informed man is the most useless bore on God's earth. What we should aim at producing is men who possess both culture and expert knowledge in some special direction. Their expert knowledge will give them the ground to start from, and their culture will lead them as deep as philosophy and as high as art."[1]

[Genuine vocational education is a comprehensively conceived and fully integrated preparation of every individual American, according to his peculiar interests, aptitudes, and abilities, for a full life in all its phases.] To transmit the culture of which Whitehead speaks, American secondary schools divide themselves into three types: The academic or traditional, the vocational or vocational-technical, and the "composite" high school that tries to be all things to all boys and girls, and is known by many names—cosmopolitan, comprehensive, community.

The traditional academic curriculum has been retained with little modification in many high schools because there has always been a considerable number of parents who have wanted their children to go to college. These youngsters must therefore be

[1] Alfred North Whitehead, *The Aims of Education, and Other Essays*, New York, New American Library, 1949, p. 1.

taught the subjects colleges require; the schools are primarily college preparatory. Under pressure the colleges have sharply modified some of their requirements. It is now a rare institution which demands Latin, and still fewer want Greek. However, modern foreign languages and formal mathematics and theoretical science are still part of the magic bodies of knowledge that admit a boy or girl to college.

In the larger cities, where the great numbers of pupils are more easily classified homogeneously than in the small community, it has been simple in the academic high schools to broaden standards and even to omit subjects for noncollege prospects. But in small rural schools with no more than two to six teachers, these teachers must be able to provide college-entrance subjects for the prospective college entrants, and the other pupils must suffer along with them regardless of their probable future careers. This is one reason for confining the present study to large and middle-sized cities where the limitations of the small school do not operate.

The vocational high school is designed to give vocational courses which will prepare young people for profitable employment—in such fields as carpentry, needle trades, farming, stenography, or machine work—as well as to educate them for civic and social responsibilities. These vocational courses should in no wise be confused with the courses in industrial arts established by the academic high schools during the period of great growth in secondary vocational instruction—well understood and appreciated by vocational educators. But no vocational educator and no well-trained industrial-arts instructor would call industrial arts vocational education.

Industrial arts has wide vocational *guidance* implications and is a suitable introduction to vocational education. Industrial arts should be given to all high school pupils for vocational-guidance purposes, and for the benefits derived from learning by doing.

School administrators should make every effort to enable industrial-arts teachers to fulfill this purpose and avoid the tendency to allow a shop—any shop—to become a resting place for nonacademic students and a refuge for disciplinary cases.

By whatever name it is known, the composite high school purports to offer *everything* provided by academic and vocational high schools, in fact, to supply *all* the educational needs of *all* the youth in the community. Whether this is, or is not a possibility, we do not know, but by patient research the Barney Project is trying to find out. It will publish further findings as soon as they are available.

However, in view of the care exercised by the New York State Department of Education in gathering its data and of the importance of the over-all problem of secondary school organization, we are printing at the end of this chapter, without any comments of our own, the findings of the Department.

WHAT SHOULD THE HIGH SCHOOL DO ABOUT ITS CURRICULUM?

Despite the fact that the original American colleges were vocational or professional institutions, we know that the academic and the later high schools that prepared for these colleges had a strictly academic curriculum. The reason was simple. The content of the college vocational program was verbal. Therefore, the preparation for it had to be verbal. We have come a long way since then. We call for secondary education of *all* American youth, and we know that those American youth will engage in all kinds of occupations—professional, commercial, industrial, agricultural, homemaking, and so on. These occupations demand all kinds of talent and all kinds of education. The secondary schools have changed, but they have not changed in the same direction. In fact, they have diverged widely in some of their aims. What can be done to bring them together, to enable them to work wholeheartedly for all young people? Such wholeheartedness does not mean *one* curriculum or *one* school. It may mean many curricula, and many different kinds of schools, but it does mean education for *all* the people.

THE PROBLEM TODAY

It is the obvious intention and probably the destiny of American people to benefit individually and collectively from the best that higher education has to offer. We are committed to being a well-educated people. This is in line with two trends already noted. One trend has been the elimination, little by little, of the traditional academic subject requirements for admission to college. The pace of elimination has been slow and is far from being complete, but it is a definite trend. The other trend is for vocational work to seep into the academic school, feebly to be sure. Nevertheless, in recognition of the fact that it is an integral part of the education of many youth, it will probably in some manner, in the long run, be given to practically *all* youth.

OUR MOST STRIKING CONCLUSION

The most striking conclusion revealed by our study is that in terms of time and content the established forty-period vocational high school offers potentially $33\frac{1}{3}$ to 40 percent more education than does the generally accepted academic high school. The academic high school fails to use this percentage of the student's time for education, and it could use this time and provide this education by giving a full day's work in a school equipped to handle the occupational phases. In effect, this conclusion challenges the American high school with the task of providing the indispensable vocational phases of sound education. For the high-school curriculum would meet the needs of many more individuals if it provided a full school day of work in an institution staffed and equipped to teach the occupational and performing arts as well as the verbal and intellectualistic phases of life.

We report the results of a comparative study of vocational and academic high school curricula, from which conclusions indicate what might be done in the immediate future to make the secondary curriculum more nearly meet the demands of all American adolescents, and what might be done toward the adaptation of the American high school to American life.

CHANGING TRENDS

The need for this study arises from what seems to be a mass of diverging educational tendencies, which when looked at more closely really converge to provide an over-all picture.

First, the old-fashioned academic high school curriculum is, as we have said, designed primarily to meet requirements for college entrance by producing the usual 15 or 16 points. More and more it has become the custom of state legislatures to prescribe the required subjects in public high schools, thus making them mandatory and leaving only a small margin of time for subjects elected in the interest of individual pupils. To add to the confusion, state legislatures, under pressure from public bodies with various interests, in recent years have imposed new subjects upon the public high schools. All have been subjects which can be taught by word of mouth or book, rather than courses of a practical nature with equipment or supply costs that make them hard to install. They have tended to crowd out practical subjects by appropriating all available instructional time.

In the 35 years since the passage of the Smith-Hughes Act in 1917, the demand for public vocational education for adolescents has been felt, resulting in a considerable amount of vocational education being added to curricula. During the same period, a much greater percentage of American youth has been attending high schools than formerly did. The size of the school population, the increased variability in pupils' attitudes, and the needs of the newer high school group have produced and are producing changes in objectives, curricula, and educational procedures.

Along with some great benefits, there have resulted much confusion, misunderstanding, and miseducation. We shall try to correct these misapprehensions by indicating the essential differences between vocational and academic curricula, to point out how a few schools in the country are approaching a solution by retaining the best features of both, and to show how many more schools could meet the situation despite the present obstacles of tradition, legislative bodies, and the inevitable lag in educational thought. What has appeared to be a controversy between the verbal educator and the practical educator could with creative thought become a reconciliation in terms of transcendent civic, social, and economic needs.

THE COMPREHENSIVE HIGH SCHOOL

The comprehensive high school[2] is a school where *all* pupils of secondary school age may have their aptitudes and interests tested and where they may learn those things for which they are well equipped and which will be of use to them in later life.

In a small community, where there can be only one high school (perhaps only one building for both elementary and high school), the "comprehensive high school" is the only physical possibility. However, the number of students is too small for any reasonable degree of homogeneous classification and the number of teachers is too small to include any but those who can each teach several academic subjects. Alert schoolmen in such communities have been forced to resort to "part-time diversified occupations" for vocational training.

Theoretically, the comprehensive high school should be a possibility and desirability for a middle-sized town and should be completely feasible in a large city. However, difficulties arise where

[2] See French, Hull, and Dodds, *American High School Administration*, New York, Rinehart & Company, 1951, pp. 110-120.

the primary aim is college admission, for the vocational courses constitute a secondary and looked-down-upon department to which the less verbally intelligent pupils are relegated. Most academically trained teachers do not understand and do not like "shops." If vocational work is injected into an academic program it often becomes so-called vocational guidance (also misapprehended as a verbal subject) plus "general occupational instruction." The indispensable training elements of vocational training are lost.

In larger cities separate general vocational high schools, or specialized high schools for particular trades, have been much more successful. Perhaps most successful have been the four-level vocational school and classes, as in Baltimore. Nevertheless, on the basic results of this study, the most successful approach to the problem appears to be through the focusing of pupil interest on the prospective vocation for approximately half the school day and on the academic, college preparatory subjects for the other half. As will be clarified, real "culture" can emerge from some such combination.

A NEW YORK STATE EDUCATION DEPARTMENT SURVEY

In its study of vocational education in New York City, the State Education Department considered comparatively the advantages and disadvantages of two types of organization—the comprehensive high school and the separate vocational school—with reference to size of community and other factors. Findings and conclusions pertinent to the present study are excerpted from the report:[3]

There is usually only one solution for providing vocational education in the city of 50,000 or less, which has only one or two high schools. This is to provide it as a department of the comprehensive

[3] *Vocational Education in the New York City High Schools*, Albany, State Education Department, 1951. Excerpts are from pp. 582-584, *passim*.

high school. In such instance, the high school administration staff must have real interest in the vocational program. This can be achieved if the desire to do so is present in the community.

In the large city, the issue is much more closely drawn. Here are found both academic high schools with vocational divisions and separate vocational schools. What are the relative merits? They depend largely on the specific conditions found in the city, such as administrative pattern of the school system, the character of the industries, the interest of employers in pre-employment vocational education, and the like. If generalized statements can be made, the following are some of the arguments for and against the separate schools:

SEPARATE VOCATIONAL SCHOOLS

Advantages	*Disadvantages*
1. The school schedule can follow that needed for vocational school work, and need not conform to an academic school schedule.	1. The guidance personnel in the feeder schools frequently give undue attention to students who plan to enter academic schools. The vocational school becomes the dumping ground for low-ability and trouble-making students.
2. Administrative and supervisory staff can be required to have background and training which is geared to vocational school needs, through certification requirements.	2. Students tend to be segregated. Often the vocational school is for boys only or for girls only, and students lose out on school relationship with the other sex.
3. The vocational program is the main function of the school, and gets primary attention.	3. Competition for students between the vocational and academic schools may not be in the best interests of the youth.
4. Relations with industry with respect to keeping courses up to date, placement of graduates, etc., seem to be somewhat more easily attained.	4. Vocational schools have often been housed in cast-off buildings and thus give
5. The whole school staff	

SEPARATE VOCATIONAL SCHOOLS

Advantages	*Disadvantages*
thinks in terms of vocational students and program, and does not have to spread its interests over a wide educational program.	the program a reputation which is hard to overcome.
6. The physical plant is frequently more functional from the standpoint of vocational work.	5. Often the facilities for health, physical education, music, etc., in the vocational school are inferior to those in the comprehensive school.
7. If the program is large enough to warrant specialization—such as graphic arts, metal trades, building trades, etc.—this can more readily be done in separate vocational schools.	6. There is less flexibility in the use of staff as compared with the comprehensive high school.

Some arguments for and against the comprehensive high school as the place for vocational education follow:

THE COMPREHENSIVE HIGH SCHOOL

Advantages	*Disadvantages*
1. The school does not have to build a separate reputation for itself. It already is an accepted American institution.	1. Sometimes the academic school day is less than six hours in length, and compromises in schedule are needed. Schedule making is more complicated.
2. A comprehensive high school with separate but adjacent vocational buildings has many advantages similar to the separate vocational school.	2. To be really comprehensive, the school should offer all the vocational activities of the city in one school. This may be impracticable.
3. The guidance service of the feeder schools tends to take the vocational work into ac-	3. Specialization in large occupational fields is hardly practicable.

Advantages	*Disadvantages*
count more readily than with separate vocational schools. 4. All students, academic and vocational, meet together in the same clubs, physical activities, etc., and thus the program tends to be more democratic. 5. More elective offerings in academic subjects, clubs, etc., are available. 6. The prestige of the staff of the vocational department may be higher in the eyes of the community.	4. Sometimes there is found the practice of shooing vocational students into classes designed for academic-minded students. 5. The administration is often more interested in the academic work than in the vocational. 6. When the vocational work is housed in a general high school building, the physical plant may not be suitable.

For the large city, the weight of advantage seems on the side of the separate school, at least for many types of programs. However, in the final analysis, the effectiveness of a vocational program, whether it is given in separate schools or in the comprehensive high school, depends on whether the leadership of the institution believes in vocational education, knows how to operate a good program, and gives it support and intelligent direction.

WHAT THE PHILOSOPHER-EDUCATORS SAY

Alfred North Whitehead was one of the outstanding philosopher-educators in this country during the second quarter of this century. Felix Frankfurter says that "from knowledge gained through the years of the personalities who in our day have affected American university life, I have for some time been convinced that no single figure has had such a pervasive influence as the late Professor Alfred North Whitehead. Certainly, so far as this applies to the country's oldest university, my statement will hardly be disputed."[4]

Whitehead came from England to Harvard in 1924. *The Aims of Education* was published in 1929. The references are to the English educational system, and in quoting we have taken the liberty of adding, in brackets, after "technical" the word "vocational," which is the American equivalent. In his definition of culture, quoted in this chapter, Whitehead takes an unreserved stand for the effectiveness of vocational education (in the fullest sense of the word "education") as motivation and fulfillment of the highest aims of education. He goes on:

But mankind is naturally specialist. One man sees a whole subject, where another can find only a few detached examples. I know that it sounds contradictory to allow for specialism in a curriculum especially designed for a broad culture. Without contradictions the world would be simpler, and perhaps duller. But I am certain that in education wherever you exclude specialism you destroy life [p. 22].

The curse that has been laid on humanity, in fable and in fact, is, that by the sweat of its brow shall it live. But reason and moral intuition have seen in this curse the foundation for advance. The early Benedictine monks *rejoiced* in their *labors* because they conceived themselves as thereby made fellow-workers with Christ.

Stripped of its theological trappings, the essential idea remains, that work should be transfused with intellectual and moral vision and thereby turned into a joy, triumphing over its weariness and its pain. Each of us will restate this abstract formulation in a more concrete shape in accordance with his private outlook. State it how you like as long as you do not lose the main point in your details. However you phrase it, it remains the sole real hope of toiling humanity; and it is in the hands of technical [vocational] *teachers* and of those who control their spheres of activity, so to mould the nation

---

[4] Preface to Alfred North Whitehead, *The Aims of Education*, New York, A Mentor Book published by The New American Library of World Literature, 1949. Quotations from Whitehead are from the same edition.

that daily it may pass to its labors in the spirit of the monks of old [pp. 53-54].

In estimating the importance of technical [vocational] education we must rise above the exclusive association of learning with book-learning. First-hand knowledge is the ultimate basis of intellectual life. To a large extent book-learning conveys second-hand information, and as such can never arise to the importance of immediate practice. Our goal is to see the immediate events of our lives as instances of our general ideas. What the learned world tends to offer is one second-hand scrap of information illustrating ideas from another second-hand scrap of information. The second-handedness of the learned world is the secret of its mediocrity. It is tame because it has never been scared by facts. The main importance of Francis Bacon's influence does not lie in any peculiar theory of inductive reasoning which he happened to express, but in the revolt against second-hand information of which he was a leader [p. 61].

If you want to understand anything, make it yourself, is a sound rule. Your faculties will be alive, your thoughts gain vividness by an immediate translation into acts. Your ideas gain that reality which comes from seeing the limits of their application [p. 63].

In conclusion, I recur to the thought of the Benedictines, who saved for mankind the vanishing civilization of the ancient world by linking together knowledge, labor, and moral energy. Our danger is to conceive practical affairs as the kingdom of evil, in which success is only possible by the extrusion of ideal aims. I believe that such a conception is a fallacy directly negatived by practical experience. In education this error takes the form of a mean view of technical [vocational] training. Our forefathers in the dark ages saved themselves by embodying high ideals in great organizations. It is our task, without servile imitation, bodily to exercise our creative energies.

"THE EDUCATION OF FREE MEN"

Horace M. Kallen in his book of this title takes a positive position on the relation of vocation to culture and the inevitability of recognizing and strengthening this relationship in the process of education. As another hypothesis for research treatment we quote several paragraphs from his striking chapter, "Of Culture and Vocation":

In sum, the humanities and the liberal arts, the crafts of magic and disputation, are gentlemanly activities, cultivated modes of behavior using up the energies of a virtuoso, whose vocation is his culture and whose product is his prestige, not his power. This prestige is his power insofar as it affects other men; and the skills that sustain it impose their authority by their appearance, not by their performance. They are completely consummatory. If man depended on this kind of knowledge alone, he would long have perished from the earth, but this kind of knowledge has ever been mixed into another kind of knowledge, to which it in fact owes much of its prestige, and whose credit it appropriates. This is the despised and menial knowledge which the workman gathers like a bee by laboring with things. It is this knowledge which is truly power. Men win it when the mind so tries things that its experiments will bring to light the operative causes of which their stuff and form are the effects. Natural philosophy is this other knowledge. This, says Bacon, "is not yet to be found un-adulterated, but is impure and corrupted by logic in the school of Aristotle; natural theology in that of Plato; by mathematics in the second school of Plato (that of Proclus and others) which ought rather to terminate natural philosophy than to generate and create it. . . ." It is only as culture and vocation can be compenetrated, so that there shall be no vocation without culture and no culture without vocation, that the schools can educate free men for a free society. It is only if they accept the different educations of men with the same democratic faith they are presumed to accept their persons, that they can bring to event the task of democratic education as Condorcet defined this task: to vindicate the equality of the different, in dignity, excellence and worth, thus making real the political equality ordained by the laws. . . . The springs of culture are agriculture, animal culture, the culture of the machines. The root of culture is vocation; the fruit of vocation is culture, alike in the institutions of society and the personal life. The glory that was Greece had to be the works and ways of men and women before it could shine out in glory. The delights of leisure which Aristotle praised as the end of life had to be the productions of servile labor before they could become the consumption of enfranchised leisure. . . . It is the relationship that creates or destroys the difference in the economy of culture, the economy that its traditionalist champions disregard. But the men and women whose vocation is music, literature, drama, painting, sculpture, dancing or architecture have always been as aware of it as their fellows, the butcher, the baker, the candlestick maker. In the advancing division of labor, any man's vocation is every other man's culture. For the dynamic of culture is free trade between vocations. Hence, the closer a man of culture gets to the vocational roots of his culture, the deeper, the more discriminating his judgment and accurate his understanding; the nearer his insight of the personality of the producer, and his fellowship with the latter's life and labors. The achievement and expression of such a fusion of sympathy and empathy, and its communication to others, is the especial vocation of the teacher. Where the fusion obtains, the invidious distinction between "useful" and "useless" knowledge lapses; what is invidious in the distinctions between fine art and commercial, sacred and profane, precious and vulgar, classic and popular, dies away. The head understands and the heart acknowledges the singularity of the worker and his workings, their symbolic transposition into other medium or other purposes, orchestrating them all to the other singularities that environ them. Such orchestration makes the culture of democracy. . . .

Kept apart from culture, vocation is servile, brutish and blind; vocational education is animal training. Kept apart from vocation, culture is parasitical, cruel and sterile; liberal education is the cultivation of futility. The education of free men requires reuniting the two so long divorced, the orchestration of the producer's knowledge which is power with the consumer's discernment which is delight.[5]

[5] Horace M. Kallen, *The Education of Free Men,* New York, Farrar, Straus & Company, 1949.

III. What's Past Is Prologue

How education got into schools

Ninety percent of American secondary education is tradition. Tradition is frozen history. This book is the story of a contemporary defrosting process; of an attempt to combine the virtues of the liberal arts (the standard high-school college preparatory program) with the essentials of vocational training. It says in effect:

A large group of boys and girls in high school (at least 10 per cent) can be and are being prepared effectively for both life and vocation, or may combine both college and vocation. This study proves that for the most intelligent top group of pupils both general and vocational education can be given in public secondary schools. High schools can give young people the full benefit of their cultural heritage and at the same time can teach them to develop their individual skills in worthy occupations. *For this group*, one school can combine the virtues of both academic and vocational high schools. The complete education of *all* other groups raises the problem of the "comprehensive" high school, which will be touched upon lightly but will be dealt with extensively in a later volume.

What is so important about the "past," and what is it "prologue" to? Historically, what is so world-shaking about this revelation regarding the 10 percent who can combine cultural and vocational education?

Several things:

First, never before, over the centuries of our civilization, have young people been invited to draw from the springs of learning and at the same time acquire the skills of a trade.

Second, never before have the people as nations and governments said to young men and women, "We, the people, want to prepare you to take your places in the world to bear the burdens both of life and of living."

Third, if the long life of man since that first glimmering of savage unconscious learning were condensed into a year of time, "schools" would have been organized only five minutes ago. Up to that moment learning was imitation, unconscious, subconscious, disordered, chaotic, formless imitation. Five minutes ago schools were started and now, when calmly considered in the light of history, they appear the most amazing of modern institutions— more amazing than government or business or industry. That *any*one can learn *any*thing, virtually *free*, in the United States, is truly astounding. In other parts of the world he cannot do so.

Fourth, for the first time in the history of education, learning, total learning—learning for the body, the soul, the emotions— learning for the entire individual, is provided as a science and an *art*. Historically speaking, until a few minutes ago there were *no* schools. Groups gathered in homes with an almost illiterate teacher. Before that, all learning was trial and error and imitation.

ACADEMIC VERSUS VOCATIONAL EDUCATION

The academic-vocational gap need not continue to exist. That it is being closed is evidenced by this study. Moreover, this brief historical sketch is written on the assumption that there must be great virtue in two kinds of learning that have lived side by side for thousands of years, even though vocational acquirements have been considered much less important and noble than academic attainments. What we here expose are the bare bones of education. They are requisite and precedent to understanding of the much debated gap.

What Is History?

More specifically, what is the history of education? It is easy enough to assume that an accurate recital of events in schools, on farms, in homes, and in churches will constitute an authentic story of education. As a matter of fact, it is the interests, emotions, reasonings, of the historian that determine how he selects and describes the events with which he is dealing. Every choice has some relation to an evaluation, to a purpose, to a standard of judgment. So the teacher of classics writes about education in one way and the teacher of trades in another. Nevertheless, we believe that the following account fully recognizes the importance of all types of education and of a balance between the individual's characteristics and the milieu in which he lives. We say that it is as impartial as scientific research and good will and a tremendous fervor for education can make it. Those readers who are interested in the hidden motives underlying the writing of history will find them in a fascinating discussion in Whitehead's *Adventures of Ideas*.[1]

Some Homely Facts in the History of Education

Viewed from our present day knowledge of highly organized schools, some homely facts emerge:

1. The History of Education is, in a sense, hardly a history of education at all. It is rather the story of how people somehow or other learned to live long before they heard of education as such. "Hit or miss" was the "method." Observation and imitation helped.

2. In the fairly recent past, home, field, factory, any place

[1] Alfred North Whitehead, *Adventures of Ideas*, Harmondsworth, Middlesex, England, Penguin Books, 1948, pp. 11-15.

where life or work was going on, was "school," if anybody had thought of calling it that. People learned through experience.

3. Primitive man learned only two things. One was to hunt, fish, make some kind of clothing, find or construct some sort of shelter; in other words, to keep himself alive. The other was to conform to whatever rituals, customs, and beliefs came under the heading of religion.

4. The first distinct educational institutions were schools for the training of priests. This was true in primitive times and continued to be so for centuries.

5. Literary education, the basis of so much that was education at all, grew out of religious education. It was the subject matter of instruction.

6. Only two or three hundred years ago (five minutes of our condensed version) the first public schools were "academic." The teachers who taught the three R's were barely literate itinerants who worked in the homes of parents and were paid in food and board and clothing.

7. The schools were private. In many parts of the world they are still private.

8. In the last fifteen seconds of our five minutes arose the vocational school, even though, from the very beginning, vocations were fundamental to sheer existence.

9. Outside of the grouping of the priests in primitive times, the first gatherings of people into what could be called schools were the medieval universities. Later came the chantry, the guild, the burgher, and other private schools.

10. *Systems* of schools were a late development. Some beginnings were made in Germany during the sixteenth century, but in France and England they were delayed until the eighteenth century.

11. Even in the nineteenth century, in the village school in Burgdorf, "where Pestalozzi was barely tolerated, even for a few

months, as assistant, the master was the ignorant village shoe-maker. Kruesi, Pestalozzi's ablest assistant, gives a very sad account of his first appointment as teacher, an office for which he had no preparation. . . . So, we find the village watchman, the bricklayer, the rope maker, the crippled soldier, the widow, or anyone whose occupation did not consume all his time or furnish him with complete living, was chosen as schoolmaster. More frequently, the convenient house which they occupied was of greater importance than their qualification as teachers."[2]

THE ACADEMIC-VOCATIONAL GAP

It is a common experience in any type of school or in any home to hear the older people say to the children, "You don't want to go to a vocational school. You have a high I.Q. You can go to college. Vocational schools are only for the dumb ones who can work only with their hands." It is common practice for principals, teachers, and counselors to urge their brightest youngsters to attend an academic high school to prepare for college, to urge the next lower group to take the easier course in an academic high school, and to tell the lowest group to go to a vocational school. The elders feel that they are giving the children the best possible advice. They are still trapped in the academic-vocational gap. Why is there such a gap? Present observation and historical groping suggest a number of possibilities, none of them lending themselves to exact proof, but all of them suggesting sound reasons:

1. Hard manual work is dirty. It produces sweat, it picks up grime, it makes one look low and untidy. Most people like to look clean and be clean.

2. Hard manual labor requires the use of heavy muscles. It makes one tired. It wears one out. It usually means standing or

[2] Paul Monroe, *A Textbook in the History of Education*, New York, The Macmillan Company, 1909, pp. 614 and 615.

walking or lifting heavy objects. It is easier to push a pen or a button, or to talk, or to think. When you have a white-collar job or, as the English say, a black-coat job, you wear a white collar or a black coat. You don't wear overalls or strip to the waist. You wear good clothes and don't look like a workman. In the professions or in white-collar jobs you meet "nicer" people. You don't have to mingle with workers. You are on a higher social plane.

3. Thinking is nobler than making or handling or backbreaking. You must be a finer person if you can earn money by thinking.

4. The poor, hard-working father wants his son to have it easier in life. He wants him to have a fine office, to wear good clothes, to use only his more delicate muscles, to make money. The poor mother wants her son to be a minister, a lawyer, or a doctor. Parents do not believe the assertion, "from shirt sleeves to shirt sleeves in three generations."

5. The technical nature of our machine age fosters the spirit of button pushing and lever pulling, of good clothes and all the other purposes of white-collar employment. Perhaps it is irrelevant, but many of us can remember how horsecar drivers and cable-car gripmen were always unprotected from the weather, were always standing, and were always pulling or hauling on the reins or the brakes. We also remember the ditchdiggers, who scooped up the earth spadeful by spadeful. Now most of these men sit on their jobs and touch lightly the levers that automatically operate the car or the motorized shovel.

6. Prejudice against vocational schools is insidious but real. Again, we point out that it arises from no ill will but rather from ignorance or misunderstanding or inherited prejudice. All the foregoing factors are at work, but we can add a few school items: (a) Some teachers have never done any manual work. They have been white-collar workers both as pupils and as teachers. It is difficult for them to conceive of bright pupils "lowering" them-

selves to the level of workers. (b) Except in unusual instances, most teachers have never belonged to unions. They have a natural aversion to work which fosters unionizing. This situation is changing. (c) Teachers desire other intellectuals to have leisure time, such as the teachers themselves have. However, this is another situation that is changing.

HISTORY OF ACADEMIC EDUCATION

Since, for many centuries, academic education was the only education consciously offered, it was education itself. Its history is briefed in the "Homely Facts." However, here are several important corollaries:

1. Up to a few hundred years ago education was the attempt of small groups of people to offer to their children a knowledge of the simple art of communication—words, simple signs, that would enable them to write and read the thoughts of others. It was essentially the three R's, on either a low level for the interchange of common, everyday thoughts or on a high level of philosophy and religion.

2. Religion was the motive for most education in the earlier days. The priests had to be literate. Later, it seemed important that the humble communicants should also be able to read—the Bible at least.

3. Such education was always private. There were no organized *systems* of public schools. Small groups and the churches provided for their own.

4. The astounding event in the history of so-called academic education has been its gradual but definite expansion into phases of life far outside of the narrow academic field. It has become rich and diversified rather than lean and academic. In fact, educators tend less and less to speak of academic education. The common term now is general education. It even talks about vocational and practical affairs and the importance of "work experience."

All of this would be encouraging if it did not smack of the "humanistic realism" of earlier days; that is to say, if it did not use other people's words about reality instead of immersing the pupil in reality itself.

5. The written histories of education deal largely with the *opinions* of the educational philosophers, and this is fair enough. Like every other human institution, education develops traditions, and traditions slow up social change. The educational philosophers have usually been the "revolutionaries" who have railed against the traditions and, in time, usually after a long time, have impressed their ideas upon the schools, and the schools have changed. So, Pestalozzi, Comenius, and Herbart never saw their ideas in practice, but their influence has been tremendous. They were all concerned with what we now call general education.

6. Teaching has rarely been practiced as an art. Great teachers have been scarce. The books tell us what good teaching is, but in actuality we see little of it; often the educational philosophers pointed the way but were themselves indifferent practitioners. Perhaps some of the best "methods" have stemmed from Froebel and the kindergarten. In fact, in the early grades of the elementary school can be found some of the best examples of intelligent and perceptive teaching. General education is responsible for much that is fine in organized education. The excellent teaching methods of the kindergarten are, however, used less and less as instruction moves up into high school and then to college.

7. General education has come a long way since the trivium and the quadrivium of the Middle Ages. We still have grammar, rhetoric, and dialectics (trivium) and arithmetic, geometry, music, and astronomy (quadrivium), but they have greatly changed in character and content and nearly all of life has been added. As reported in the latest volume of this type of education,[3] general

[3] B. Lamar Johnson, *General Education in Action*, Washington, D. C., American Council on Education, 1952.

education includes democratic citizenship, sound moral and spiritual values, reading and writing, mathematical and mechanical skills, critical thinking, cultural heritage, biological and physical environment, mental and physical health, personal and social adjustments, home and family life, vocational adjustments, and creative activity.

8. Whatever the shortcomings of general education may be (and, as with any type of education, they are many), in the long struggle of man to better himself he has made tremendous strides in developing subject matter and methods and institutions and teachers to convey past culture and a creative future to the ever-changing new generation. Any other type of education, certainly vocational education, must draw from this rich treasure of experience for much of its technique and for some of its content. Indeed, for certain young people general and vocational education may well be combined in such a way as to enhance the value of both.

HISTORY OF VOCATIONAL EDUCATION

As long as men have wanted beautifully or skillfully made objects, there have been craftsmen. And as long as there have been craftsmen, there has been some kind of vocational education. But crafts, arts, and occupations have been learned—and, largely, are still learned—on the job. Learning has been a by-product of living. Somehow or other, the work of the world has been done without the conscious intervention of the educator.

The story of vocational education is full of paradoxes. The need for such training grew out of civilized man's increasingly complicated life; yet the more the highly cultured free Greeks depended on craftsmen for comfort and pleasure, the more they tended to scorn the slaves who produced them. And much later many of the men who contributed so much to the recognition of manual training and its benefits to youth were often idealists who were doomed to failure in more practical endeavor.

Yet almost since the dawn of time some societies have dignified crafts and protected them with statutes. The Talmud directed the Jews: "As it is your duty to teach your son the law, teach him a trade. . . . Disobedience to this ordinance exposes one to just contempt for thereby the social conditions of all are endangered." But the father taught the trade at home. School meant reading and writing.

The Babylonian Code of Hammurabi (2250 B.C.) presaged some of the regulations of the medieval guilds: "If an artisan take a son for adoption and teach him his handicraft, one may not bring claim against him. If he do not teach him his handicraft, that adopted son may return to his father's house."

The early Christians, in their eagerness to escape worldly vanities and attain the humility of the Church Fathers, plunged into manual labor. The Benedictine Rule of the sixth century allotted seven hours a day to manual labor—and as many to the praise of God. And especially as monasteries took over the publishing of books, they became the centers for vocational as well as all higher education. But teaching was casual and unpremeditated. The primary motive was not job efficiency but moral prophylaxis.

EXPERIENCE AND IMITATION

Vocational education, if it could be called education, started with experience and imitation, just as any other type of education must have started. Call it hit or miss, trial and error, or stealing the job, it is the way that people have learned to survive. Conscious education came much later.

Centuries later, when men employed a number of workers, a boss or an older employee showed the younger worker how to do his job. And again, the new employee imitated the motions of the older one. Always showing, observation, imitation. All this was done by individuals on a small scale, without organization, as a private venture. However, there came a time when the em-

ployers organized into associations and gave instruction to groups
of men who were called apprentices.

The Role of the Guilds

Then, in the Middle Ages, guilds were becoming a part of
secular life, even as the medieval universities were making the
professions education-conscious. With the Renaissance and its
urbanizing influences, guilds and their apprenticeship systems provided the main educational institute for the middle class. The
methods of guild teaching varied from craft to craft and from
country to country. There were usually four classifications in the
guild, though a man might stay in one of the lower ones for life
or—especially if he were a master's son—skip a step or two on
his way up the ladder. The classifications were apprentice (*gar-
çon*), journeyman (*valet*), craftsman working under orders
(*compagnon*), and master with full rights in the guild and running his own business (*serviteur*). However, some guilds did not
have these classes.

The idyllic picture, as presented, for example, in Richard Wag-
ner's *Die Meistersinger von Nürnberg*, of the workman beside
his master sharing his table, his roof, and his labor, walking with
him in public processions and public ceremonies, rarely existed,
according to Georges Renard, except in the building trades. The
jealousies between apprentices, who represented cheap labor, and
the journeymen and *compagnons*, who were paid at least in part
with money, and the master's desire to limit expert competition,
did not enhance the system. The privileges given a master's son
also tended to increase guild monopoly and keep journeymen in
their niches. Even so, the system had happy aspects. Medieval
women, though often in a position of subjugation and not permitted by guild laws to become masters, were in some areas ac-
corded considerable economic independence. Some cities had fe-
male guilds, such as those of the silkworkers, the gold-thread

workers, and others in the dressmaking industry. And there were also mixed guilds, such as the bakers', where the wife had the right to carry on her master-husband's workshop after his death. Benefit clubs, also a feature of guilds, insisted on thrift and careful, systematic teaching.

A typical apprenticeship agreement would run (with variations) something like this: A master, of good life and character, endowed by patience and approved by guild officers, would take on ten or twelve apprentices for instruction for six, eight, ten, or twelve years. During a two-week trial period, either master or boy could back out. The apprentice's guardians probably paid a minimum fee in corn, bread, or money and in return the master provided the youth with food, lodging, clothes, washing, and light as well as instruction. The apprentice took an oath to be industrious and obedient and to work for no other master. The master promised to teach the lad the secrets of the craft and treat him "well and decently in sickness as in health." (One master was given the privilege of correcting and beating his apprentice "short of drawing blood.") If the apprentice ran away, his place was kept open for a specified period of time (in one case 26 weeks), and if he came back he was punished and retained. After three such escapades he was likely to be dismissed, his parents required to indemnify the master, and the boy not permitted to return to his abandoned craft. The guild protected the apprentices' rights, as attested by cases in which apprentices were set at liberty after being treated inhumanly by masters.

EXPERIMENTS IN THE VOCATIONAL APPROACH

After the honest and effective apprentice program of the guild many attempts were made to capitalize upon the vocational approach without actually giving specific and profitable training in vocational skill. Each of these attempts had its specific value, but none of them met the problem head on.

In the early part of the nineteenth century many mechanic institutes were organized in England. After a day in the factories, workers would attend these institutes in the evenings. Courses were given to supplement and explain the processes in which they had been engaged during the day. Somewhat later similar institutes were organized in New York and other American cities. Today, throughout the country, there are public evening trade schools where workers may obtain valuable instruction in their trades. The combination of working experience on the job and classroom and shop instruction in the school is a wholesome, upgrading procedure.

In the late nineteenth century, much interest was aroused in the educational values of manual training. Especially in Sweden, England, and the United States classes were organized as part of the regular elementary school curriculum. However, these were not intended to prepare for or even guide into a trade, but rather to confer upon the youngsters the psychological benefits of hand work. Manual training was a phase of general education.

Growing out of the manual training idea, but with much more realistic objectives, industrial arts courses have been set up in thousands of elementary, junior high, and high schools throughout the United States. This again is not vocational education, but is just as important. A good industrial arts course acquaints the pupil with the industrial organization of his country, gives him elementary skills in the handling of various kinds of media (wood, metal, clay, plastics), and this combination of knowledge and skill helps him to make a wise choice, tentative though it may be, of a future vocation.

Another approach to vocational education was the continuation school in Germany, the value of which was recognized in the United States in 1917 with the establishment of continuation schools in most of the 48 states. While the movement was a tremendous step toward real vocational education, it was, for the most part, not vocational education itself. True, in a few of the largest cities of both the United States and Germany, the continuation schools gave direct shop instruction. However, for the most part, the schools relied on the work experience of the pupil for training and skill, and supplemented this, during four or eight hours a week, with the latest technical knowledge and some instruction in English and the social studies. These schools had a tremendous influence upon the later development of full-time day schools, which became more and more important as one state after another raised its compulsory full-time age from 14 to 16 years. As part of the evolutionary process of clarifying and standardizing full-time vocational education, the continuation schools played an important role.

While the continuation school in Germany has often been lauded as a praiseworthy effort in vocational education, it was and is actually only for the 50% to 90% of the children of high school age who can never qualify for admission to high school and must work after they are 14 years of age. In the United States the problem has been largely solved by the raising of the compulsory full-time age to 16. However, between the 16th and 18th years there is much to be done in the way of providing full-time vocational education or half-time cooperative education.

When mental defectives have been segregated in schools and it has proved impractical to teach them symbols from books, it has proved beneficial to teach them trades. It was often said during the latter part of the nineteenth century that if you wanted to learn a trade, the best way was to have yourself committed to a reformatory. Delinquents, as well as those who act normally toward society, benefit from a well-balanced program of vocational and general education.

FULL-TIME VOCATIONAL EDUCATION

The amazing thing about vocational education in the United States, during the first half of the twentieth century, has been the development of vocational high schools on the secondary level.

For the first time American communities have met head on the problem of preparing youth for the vocations of the age. They have done it largely through schools devoted half time to practical shop work and half time to related and general subjects. These schools have had amazing success. However, the question raised and answered by this study is, Have either the specialized vocational schools or the college preparatory academic schools done this job adequately for those pupils who are of the intelligence and temperament congenial to both types of school? The answer to this question should throw a brilliant light on the task of secondary schools, not only with this special group, but with the entire high school age group. The community high school that serves *all* the youth and has provided for *all* their educational needs is commonly called the comprehensive high school—a type of school that is the subject of current research by the Barney Project.

VOCATIONAL EDUCATION BECOMES AN ART

Fundamentals of education are always the same. They derive from the nature of the child. Since children differ so markedly from each other, these fundamentals present many complexities. However, schoolmen and psychologists have made great strides in understanding the nature of learning. The findings can be applied to many different kinds of subject matter. Nevertheless, vocational education gives rise to many peculiar problems to which practical educators have been alert. Over the years, teachers and directors and principals in vocational schools have done much to convert the early processes—imitation, showing, observation—to expert methods that include dynamic demonstration, effective visual and auditory aids, keen industrial analysis, skillfully written textbooks, and dramatic presentations. In other words, just as the professions of law and medicine have derived from early arbitrary and haphazard methods into highly systematized and scientifically correct procedures, so the vocational educator has left behind the easy imitative methods of primitive times and has arrived at procedures that deserve to be called an art. This is of especial importance when, within the range of subjects included in a vocational curriculum, there are those whose content is already designated as art—graphic, plastic, and performing.

THE PARALLEL BETWEEN GENERAL AND VOCATIONAL EDUCATION

Over the centuries, as in general education, the curriculum of vocational education has expanded tremendously, from the industrial and agricultural occupations to the professions, architecture, engineering, law, and the ministry. Whereas these vocations began with simple, unskilled movements and the most ordinary bits of common knowledge, they have all developed into highly complex, precise, sophisticated, even noble vocations. The schools that train for them must teach the "know-why" as well as the "know-how"—the related and technical knowledge— along with a generous proportion of related and cultural subjects. As any surgeon will tell you, he must first of all be an excellent mechanic. As any artist will tell you, he must be first of all a competent technician. All these know-why qualifications edge up closely to those supposedly acquired through general education, making it quite obvious that the task of any school in developing such qualifications must be closely examined so that there may be agreement as to the extent to which general education and vocational education supplement each other.

EDUCATION IS LIFE

Vocational education is not job training. It is not perfection of skills. It is not tricks of the trade. It is not haggling in the marketplace, wrangling in law courts, breaking of soil, or binding of wounds. It is all of these, but it is much more. It is a creative spirit in the mechanic, service rendered by the merchant, justice won by the prosecutor, food raised by the farmer, and life saved by the doctor. It is attitudes, emotions, ethics, conduct, language, and beauty—those attributes that transform jobs into vocations and men and women into their neighbors' keepers and into citizens of the world. It is to "walk worthy of the vocation wherewith ye are called."

Of all the things that surround a man the only ones that constitute his real environment are those that make him change his mind or change his words or change the direction in which he is moving. When we say a person is "oblivious of his surroundings," we are saying that he has no environment. So, in school, how often have we been "oblivious"—of the teacher's voice, of the chalk marks on the blackboard, of the hieroglyphics in the mathematics book, all the while intent upon the real environment, the adventure story under the desk. Vocational education provides not only a genuine environment in which a person changes because he is concerned with it, but one which is contrived and directed so as to produce positive values. In other words, when life is interesting we pay attention. Life *is* interesting, particularly when it means doing, aiming toward a goal, achieving a career, being a real person.

Being *for* life, vocational education assumes the existence *of* life. Vocational education is not something presented to or done for young people or for men and women. It is an opportunity for vibrant, eager, growing human beings to do something they want to do for themselves. To use the traditional phrase, it does not have to educe activity. It merely touches off a spark. It releases latent energy. It gives the living a chance to live.[4]

VOCATIONAL EDUCATION AS RELATED TO WORK

Patently, work is much more than "work," and knowing *how* to work is much more than knowing how to perform an operation. In all its radiations work is vocation, life with a purpose. So, vocational education is much more than knowing how to work, it is education with a purpose, for a purpose. Vocational education is learning how to work, but it is learning how to work in a milieu, among people, with people, for people. It is learning how to live with other workers, at home, at play, and in the community. It is learning to live efficiently

[4] Franklin J. Keller, *Principles of Vocational Education*, Boston, D. C. Heath & Company, 1948, p. 4.

and morally. It is *everybody* learning to work, first of all, *you*, your butcher, your baker, your electric light maker, your professor, your barber, your doctor, your favorite movie actor, your clergyman, the architect who planned your house, the maid who keeps it tidy, and the plumber who made America sanitary. Then all the others, some of whom you have never seen and therefore do not know so well—the aitch-bone breaker, alley boy, ballyhoo man, animated-cartoon artist, and the delayed-bill-analysis-clerk, final touch-up man, pigs' feet boner, anthropologist, ash man, pants maker, strip-tease artist, and sweeper.

In its manual and technical phases, vocational education is teaching others how to work. In the rise from savagery to civilization, people have learned to work in many different ways. At first they must have learned by accident, the Lamb-roast-pig method. Down through the ages, the most popular method has been trial and error, mostly error—the auto-mechanic-learning-on-your-car. Slaves learned under the whiplash, duller folk often learn best when they are "yelled at." Average people learn by being told how and by being shown. Bright boys and girls need only watch the expert and then imitate. They learn by observation and doing.

It is obvious that, through these casual, fortuitous methods, all adult persons who earn a living must have received some kind of vocational education. Planned, organized vocational education comes late in the history of work. Apprenticeship is one of the early forms, the public vocational school one of the latest.

Vocational education has generally been identified with the manual and technical phases, and very naturally so. For vocational education, as a means of human development, has usually been a protest against neglect, and in its earlier, organized phases, was almost solely a teaching of manipulative ability. The history of what has been known as vocational education is largely the story of men and women who have recognized the importance of teaching people how to perform manual operations well. The history of what has been called professional education has included better performance but has emphasized theory, the scientific basis, the knowing *why* as well as *how*. Modern vocational education for all vocations—industrial, agricultural, commercial, professional—comprises not only performance and theory but the whole life of the worker. The history of vocational education is revealing even in as brief a treatment as the following must be. In truth, it is more a history of opinion than accomplishment, but it clears the way for understanding.[5]

WHAT HAS HISTORY TAUGHT US?

Only in recent times, certainly never before in the high schools, have we consciously endeavored to prepare young people simultaneously for a trade and for college. Education for life is as old as life, but schools for life are comparatively modern affairs. Schools of occupations were developed only yesterday, and even today they are largely suspect by the general educators.

Insofar as there have been endeavors in both fields they have existed apart. Ignorance, prejudice, emotion, each has played its part. Little desire for rapprochement has been shown. Yet, little by little, the general educations have taken in segments of vocational education and vocational educations have infiltrated the cultural area.

The result is that we have in the United States at least twelve high schools from which boys and girls may graduate into a skilled occupation or into a liberal or technical arts college. No passing, no conditions, just graduate and enter.

There has been practically nothing in print to show that it has been happening. Stating it theoretically but conclusively, Edgar Dale tells the story:[6]

If you read the speeches of college presidents and deans, you will find that they have come out unequivocally for a broad education and against a narrow education. They are for general education and against a highly specialized or specific education. They are against vocationalism, and for an education that is good for everybody.

I am for these things, too, even though I'm not quite sure what they mean. But I submit that we are not reaching this kind of objec-

[5] *Op. cit.*, pp. 35-36.
[6] *The News Letter*, Bureau of Educational Research, Ohio State University, April, 1951.

tive in much of our college teaching. I'd like to discuss general education and see if there isn't some way in which we can use films or
radio or other audio-visual materials to achieve a more effective
general education.

Let us examine the word general. Too often we mistakenly use it
as meaning not specific. *Yet a general education that has not been
specific is no more possible than being a man before you have been
a boy.* Specificity and generality are little boys and big men.

Some say that in general education we want to get away from
hundreds of specifics. You can't do it by giving up specifics or con-
creteness or illustration. *The only way to move away from specifics
is to build them into generalizations.* As William James once said:
*"We can only see as far into a generalization as our knowledge of its
details extends."*

But specificity does not automatically move into generality. Specifics
become fruitful generalizations because we make them so; we
purposely work for generalization.

We cannot master generalizations in the same way that we can
master specifics. A little vocational trick can be easily mastered because it is usually quite concrete and specific. You can quickly learn
to tie a knot in a certain way or do a repetitive operation with a
machine, as in a factory. The beginning and end of the process is
"at hand," is "visible." It is a closed experience as far as one's responsibility is concerned.

But the difference between the specific and the general is that the
general is always an open-ended, never a closed event. It has a
*growing edge. We might better speak of generalized education rather
than general education,* since *we should emphasize the process rather
than the product.*

The difference between a narrow and a broad education is that in
the former you get things over with. You finish with them. You
circumscribe the range of connections with other life experience. Man
as generalizer, however, sees all activities as *"suffused with suggestive-
ness"* (in Whitehead's phrase).

You cannot add up specifics to get a generalization. You must
integrate them, put them into a pattern, reconstruct them. Otherwise
you're in the dilemma of the fellow who said that he could read the

words all right but the sentences bothered him a lot. (We would add to these means—vocational education.)

Specificity, therefore, is important and inescapable. It is not anti-thetical to general education but corollary and anterior to it. The fact that an experience is a narrow one at this time is not unfavorable as far as later generalization is concerned. The issue is the dynamic quality of the experience itself. Is narrowness moving into broadness, is specificity moving toward generality? These are the questions to be asked.

History has taught us that life is an experience, it is a flow, through time, a duration, a many-colored episode in eternity. What comes out of this experience is a myriad of specifics which we, in all our human frailty, must generalize. And upon these generalizations we perform new specific acts—we continue to partake of life.

Now let us see what twelve schools in the United States do to carry on this historical imperative.

IV. The Knowers vs. the Doers

*How much and what kind of vocational education
at what age?*

How much and what kind of vocational education at what age? The answer grows out of a careful analysis of what has already been done in public high schools. Research is its core. It is a forerunner to more intensive research that will provide answers for all pupils of high school age.

However, as in all education, no new fact is learned, no new principle is understood, except in the light of the learner's previous experience. Today's educator is indebted to all his predecessors and all his colleagues for *their* experiences. In Chapter III history has spoken. In the present chapter we hear from the modern educator. We too "are compassed about with a cloud of witnesses" who have dared and done in faith, so "let us run with patience the race that is set for us."

This is a chapter of quotations, a chapter of testimony of worthy witnesses, the kind of testimony that is essential for the evaluation of new facts. Long as some of the excerpts are, they are but fragments of the volumes that have been written on secondary education. Along with our editorial comment, they provide a background of understanding and interpretation.

Books on education and researches in it are legion. Theories of education are few, some in sharp opposition one with another.

Out of a multitude of investigations, experiments, theories, should emerge some satisfactory proposal for a sound means of preparing young people for life—*all* of life. But life changes, people change, processes change, and research goes on. Satisfaction lies only in continuous adaptation to such changes.

Examination of many texts in the field of secondary education has been without profit as to the type of data we are seeking. The available texts do give a broad view of high school curricula, describing various approaches to the organization of courses of study—the core curriculum, the common learnings plan, the integrated course, the project method, and the traditional individual subject curriculum.[1] However, detailed analyses of particular school programs throughout the country are lacking. Their very absence brought about this study. We think the results are truly meaningful.

KNOWING VERSUS DOING

First of all, there must be recognized the long struggle, with no definite end in sight, between those who have exalted "knowing" and those who have sung the virtues of "doing." So far as formal education is concerned, the balance has always hung heavy on the side of "knowers." Only sporadically have the "doers" attained to any ascendance. For curriculum purposes, there seem to be only three basic ideas. You can learn (1) to know and be cultured; (2) to work, to do things and be a worker; (3) to do better those things that are common to family and social life, to acquire common learnings. As we shall see, there are those who would combine all three of these objectives into a curriculum calculated to fit each individual into a changing

[1] For a recent commendable approach, see Hollis L. Caswell and associates, *Curriculum Improvement*, New York, Bureau of Publications, Teachers College, Columbia University, 1950.

society. However, in actual practice this kind of curriculum is rare.

Does a curriculum purvey knowledge? Surely it does—in part. But what is knowledge? That it can be more—or less—than useful for sound human development is pointedly set forth by Kallen. *Delicate* knowledge is to knowledge what court dress is to the body. *Fantastic* knowledge is personal pretension to power over nature. The purpose of *contentious* knowledge is power over men. Unquestionably this is an extreme view, but it sets the scene for the evaluation of knowledge, of true knowledge, as an essential element in education.

Knowing is either an autonomous activity like a spider's spinning his web, or such a passional contortion of things and their ways, as to enfold them all in the misleading disguises of our fantasy. The knowledge we so pride ourselves on is merely delicate, or fantastic or contentious. Delicate knowledge is the body of accomplishments that mark the gentleman and courtier; it is the outcome of concern with *litterae humaniores* and the liberal arts. It is to the mind what court dress is to the body. Decorative, ceremonial, ostentatious, a mode of what Veblen called conspicuous consumption. Fantastic knowledge is not so much personal accomplishment as personal pretensions to power over nature. Bacon says it apes true knowledge; magic, alchemy and astrology are its outstanding representatives. Contentious knowledge is even more personal in its pretensions than the fantastic. Its purpose is power over men. Its method of getting that power is the scholastic procedure, as that implements or modifies the logic of Aristotle. Assuming that the mind already possesses or is not aware of the universal truth of reason and nature, the contentious man undertakes to elicit it dialectically and compel others to accept it by demonstrative proof or by his powers of persuasion. He is concerned only with the already-known and the ready-made. His a prioris rule out discovery and invention, yet the a priori is the father of life. With all its prestige it cannot reach to the causes of things, although "it is a correct position that true knowledge is a knowledge of causes." With a prioris the contentious man may win an argument, but cannot control an event. It is rather a weapon of what Veblen called exploit, like a duelist's sword, and the causes that it emphasizes, those "barren virgins," the final causes, corrupt rather than advance the sciences.[2]

EARN A LIVING, LIVE A LIFE

If a school curriculum is to help the individual to do better those things which he will do anyway, or—what is better—to do better things better, such a curriculum must be built up on a basis of actuality. What do people do from day to day? What knowledge and skills do they need to do it more effectively and more purposefully?

A frequently uttered oblique criticism of a vocational education takes the form: It is not enough to learn to earn a living, one must learn to live a life. In the light of the foregoing analysis, no such clearcut dichotomy seems tenable. Assuming the necessity for purposeful living, what should those purposes be? Certainly each individual is obligated to secure his own personal development—subsistence, status, and ultimately, happiness. On the other hand, as a member of a community, he is obligated to render service to others, to live with his fellow men, to contribute to their development along with his own. He must "work" for others as well as for himself. Now, unless he is willing to live a double life, become a dual personality, spend half his time in toil, "earning a living," the other half in pleasure, "living a life," such a separation of activities is impossible, certainly not desirable, and for purposes of education, quite untenable. In actual adult life these two phases of living shade one into the other. It is only the rare, extreme deviate who derives absolutely no pleasure from his work and injects none of his work into his leisure.

Consider what a man does on a normal "work" day. For approximately 12 hours all his moves and all his thoughts are conditioned by his work. From the blast of the alarm clock and his slow-growing consciousness of another world to the time he enters his front door for the evening meal, he is literally at work. He washes, dresses, eats breakfast, walks to the train, rides for miles, walks again, enters the factory or office, all in preparation for the work of the day. He associates with fellow workers all day, even at lunch, and in the

[2] Horace M. Kallen, *The Education of Free Men*, New York, Farrar, Straus & Company, 1949, p. 295.

evening reverses the morning's procedure. At home he is likely to reminisce about the day's work, cheerfully or resentfully, and then visit or entertain friends who have been acquired through work associations. There is more talk about work or workers. The physical welfare, the mental and emotional happiness of wife and children are determined by the breadwinner's work. They are likely to talk about it a great deal. Meetings of trade associations or unions at home, and in other cities, provide much of the social milieu. If the worker is a farmer, work and "life" become almost indistinguishable.

True, there are movies, theaters, concerts, newspapers, magazines, books, games, and outings, which have no direct relation to the job, and yet, to suppose that the capacity to enjoy life in these so-called cultural areas is not conditioned, or unconditioned by work activities during the major time period of life, is to be utterly unrealistic. In any case, if the activities and human associations of the work period are congenial, the worker will live twice as much and twice as well as he will if they are not. And, of course, there immediately arises the question towards which later chapters will be directed: For which and for how much, of these activities, in terms of time consumed and of laudable purpose implied, is organized education necessary?

Finally, with reference to purpose, it is significant to note the tremendous role it has played in the history of mankind. The teleological aspect of philosophy has always been the most baffling. It is the essence of theology and, for many, the prime mover in religion. The scientific age staved it off for a while, but more recently scientists have been on the trail of purpose. Biologists have been seeking it in the gene or chromosome. An endocrinologist looks "behind the universe" to explain glands. The Dartmouth Eye Institute suspects "purpose" in the structure of the eye. If things have purpose, certainly men have purpose. It is something they "work" for.[3]

THE LEISURE-CLASS IDEAL IN EDUCATION

No upper-class person of wealth or education thinks of sending his son to a trade school. Every taxicab driver envisions the day when his boy will graduate from a liberal arts college. Like it or not, vocational education is looked down upon except when

[3] Franklin J. Keller, *Principles of Vocational Education*, Boston, D. C. Heath & Company, 1948, pp. 13-14.

it becomes professional, as in law, medicine, the ministry, or engineering. There are several explanations, not all of which have stemmed from Aristotle, but they do rest mainly on the ancient dualism of work and leisure. The typical college graduate has to work by the sweat of his brow (even if he wears a white collar), but his liberal arts preparation is mainly for his leisure moments. The learning of verbal and mathematical symbols is an ancient and honorable practice and is still honorable. In the latter scientific, technical, and industrial days there has been a trend through vocational education, but the general regard for such education still lags far behind. Brubacher tells the story:

In ancient societies leisure was not something each man earned as a result of labor. Rather was it the possession, the badge of distinction, of a particular class in society. This class, the aristocracy or nobility, had leisure because they were supported by the economic toil of another class—slaves in the ancient world, serfs in the medieval one. In addition, the upper class had continuous leisure while the lower class lived a life of unremitting toil.

There was no middle ground in this dichotomous class structure of ancient times. True, there were artisans and tradesmen, who worked as freemen rather than as slaves and who accepted pay for their services. Yet these men were degraded by the fact that there were many skilled slaves with whom they were in competition. But above all, they were rendered servile by the fact that they worked with their hands. Thus, Spartans were forbidden to learn a trade, and Aristotle advised giving one up as soon as possible if one were intent upon virtue. To accept pay for one's services did not distinguish one from being a slave. It was only further proof of not being "wellborn" and of being incapacitated to pursue virtue because motivated by gain. Thus social class was a matter of status. One was born to a life of leisure or to a life of toil. There was practically no social mobility by which one might improve his social status.

From this social-economic structure, profound educational consequences developed. The kind of education which fitted for the profitable use of leisure obviously pointed in a widely different direction from that which fitted for labor with one's hands. No formal education whatever was necessary for those who labored with their hands. For centuries all that they needed to know could be learned informally in the course of their daily tasks. On the whole, this was as true of artisans and tradesmen as of those who labored on the land. For the upper class formal education was both a necessity and a luxury. Training in the symbols of written language was necessary to give them access to the recorded culture. While this training was indispensable to the priestly caste, it was only varyingly useful to those engaged in civil administration. Over and above those who performed these functions of an upper class were a few who indulged in the luxury of learning verbal and mathematical symbols for their own sake.

The kinds of education befitting these two social classes also had a deeper rationale. Thus Aristotle found justification for existing social stratification in man's psychological nature. In this nature he noted two characteristics, the appetitive and the reasonable. To the higher, or reasonable, of course, was given direction and control over the lower, or appetitive. To these two characteristics of the individual corresponded the two classes of society. Since the upper class held the offices in society that were directive and controlling their proper education was the education of the mind. Since the lower class corresponded to the appetitive, their proper education was of the body. The one was an education in thinking, the other an education in doing, the one literary, the other manual. The one demanded leisure for the development of ideas, and the other opportunity for work. Herein lay an early criterion for evaluating education. The more purely mental and educational activity, the more valuable. Indeed, the most profitable use of leisure was regarded as the pursuit of knowledge for its own sake, anciently, the discipline of liberal education.

Aristotle's analysis of the nature of the individual and of society seemed so reasonable that the educational corollaries based thereon dominated the history of education down to modern times. An interesting outcropping of this early stratum of educational history occurred in the late medieval period. The medieval agrarian economy was also socially dichotomous. The feudal system was a hierarchy of various levels; the fundamental distinction was that between the landed nobility and the serfs. It is not surprising, therefore, to find perpetuation in feudal society of the distinction between work and leisure or at least between using one's hands to work and using them to fight.

Thus, among late medieval studies philosophy, theology, and logic ranked first in prestige because of their purely mental character. Law and medicine were included within the sphere of respectability only because the element of manual service to others was less evident than in handicraft industry. But medical education was on a lower plane than legal education because it was more concerned with the body than with the mind. Thus, too, the fine arts stood below the liberal ones because of the element of manual dexterity involved in their mastery. And even in the liberal arts there existed a hierarchy predicated on the dualism of mind and body as allied to that of work and leisure and arising from social stratification. The trivium of logic, grammar, and rhetoric outranked the quadrivium of music, arithmetic, geometry, and astronomy. . . .

Great and genuine as the success of the middle class has been with the aid of the Industrial Revolution, its success in projecting its culture patterns into American education was not complete. The traditional aristocratic leisure-class ideal of education still held key points of the educational front. Most notably it was entrenched in the liberal-arts college. *There a sturdy attempt was still being made in the nineteenth and twentieth centuries to maintain the superiority of cultural education, the education of the intellect for its own sake, over vocational education.* The badge of this education, the bachelor of arts degree, had a definite prestige value over all other bachelors' degrees. Higher education in such fields as technology and teaching consequently suffered in comparison because of their more practical character. Moreover, from the citadel of the college, the cultural ideal of education tended to exercise a tyranny over the curricula of secondary schools. There the college-preparatory course topped a hierarchy that tapered down to technical and commercial courses.[4]

Despite the scholarly nature of Brubacher's book and its valiant attempts to present the vocational education problem in the light of its history, he closes his chapter on secondary education with a conclusion of the American Youth Commission (to which

[4] John S. Brubacher, *A History of the Problems of Education*, New York, McGraw-Hill Book Company, 1947, pp. 80 and 90.

he apparently gives consent) to the effect that the prime function of the secondary school is to provide a liberal education:

The great economic depression of 1929 gave further importance to the secondary school as a place for liberal or general education, and this in spite of the current pragmatic approach to the high school curriculum and *in spite of its large cargo of vocational subjects.* Unemployed youth presented such a serious problem at that time that a special study was made of their social and educational needs. The American Youth Commission, after examining the problem from all angles, reported that, while 70 per cent of youth wished to enter white-collar occupations, the country could absorb only about 12 per cent in this way. Now, if 50 to 75 per cent of all remaining jobs required little or no technical training, *the great majority of high school youth was not going to need to go to high school to prepare for a job.* The vocational character of the high school's aim to prepare for life would therefore have to be *radically revised.* The conclusion that the commission drew was that *"the prime function, therefore, of universal secondary education is to provide liberal education for the common life of the whole population."*[5]

THE ATTITUDE TOWARD WORK: FOSTERING INTERNAL UNITY IN MAN

Opposed to the leisure-class ideal is the reverence for activity, work, doing, the unity, wholeness, integrity of man. This could not be more clearly or forcefully stated than it is by Jacques Maritain, in his book, *Education at the Crossroads*:

The whole work of education and teaching must tend to unify, not to spread it out; *it must strive to foster internal unity in man.*

This means that from the very start, and, as far as possible, all through the years of youth, hands and mind should be at work together. (This point has been made particularly clear by modern pedagogy as regards childhood. It is also valid for youth.) The importance of manual work accompanying the education of the mind during the high school and college training is more and more recognized. There is no place closer to man than a workshop, and

[5] Brubacher, *op. cit.*, p. 453.

the intelligence of a man is not only in his head, but in his fingers, too. Not only does manual work further psychological equilibrium, but it also furthers ingenuity and accuracy of the mind, and is the prime basis of artistic activity. Occasionally—and the state of the world during and after the present war will perhaps require imperatively such a task—youth might cooperate in many kinds of labor, harvesting, for instance, needed for the common welfare. But as a rule, and from the educational point of view, it is craftsman's labor—and also, for the sake of our mechanical age, mechanical and constructive dexterity—that should constitute the manual training of which I am speaking. I should like to add that this emphasis on manual work in education seems to me to correspond to a general characteristic of the world of tomorrow, where the dignity of work will probably be more clearly recognized, and the social cleavage between *Homo faber* and *Homo sapiens* done away with.

A second implication of the rule we are discussing [what Maritain calls "the third rule"] is that education and teaching must start with *experience,* in order to complete themselves with reason. This is obvious and needs no elucidation, save perhaps that special stress should be laid upon the second part of the statement, in an age where an empiricist philosophy often makes capital out of experience, and the highest functions of reason and the insights of abstract thought are disregarded. To be sure, sense-experience is the very origin of all our nature. Modern methods are perfectly aware of that, especially with children. The point, however, is to disengage from experience the rational and necessary connections with which that experience is pregnant, and which become visible only by means of abstraction and universal concepts, and in the light of the intuitive first principles of reason. Thus knowledge and science arise from experience. *Neither those empiricists who despise abstract reason, logic, and the conceptual insights of intelligence, nor those rationalists who ignore experience, are integrated minds.* Education must inspire eagerness both for experience and for reason, teach reason to base itself on facts and experience to realize itself in rational knowledge, grounded on principles, looking at the *raisons d'etre,* causes and ends, and grasping reality in terms of how and why.[6]

[6] Jacques Maritain, *Education at the Crossroads*, New Haven, Yale University Press, 1943, pp. 45, 46, and 47.

With regard to work, which he considers under the head of
"the fourth fundamental disposition," a term which need be
explained here only in the following words, Maritain writes:

> The fourth fundamental disposition concerns the sense of *a job
> well done*, for next to the attitude toward existence there is nothing
> more basic in man's psychic life than the attitude toward work. I do
> not mean by this the habit of being hard working. I am aware that
> laziness, as well as pride, is natural to us. Moreover laziness in children
> is often not real laziness but only an absorption of the mind with the
> workings of vegetative growth or psychophysical hardships. I am
> speaking of something deeper and more human, a respect for the job
> to be done, a feeling of faithfulness and responsibility regarding it. A
> lazy man, a poet if you will, may display, when he happens to work,
> the most passionate attachment to the inner requirements of his work.
> I am convinced that *when this fundamental disposition, which is the
> first natural move toward self-discipline, this probity in regard to
> work is marred, an essential basis of human morality is lacking.*[7]

WHAT IS KNOWING? WHAT IS DOING? WHAT THE
EDUCATORS SAY

The books on vocational education have been few. For reasons
given by Brubacher the general educators have been slow to
credit vocational education with the power of developing the
young. Teacher training has been overwhelmingly academic.
Academic teachers have spawned more academic teachers, and
vocational education has been forced to set itself up as a
separate entity.

However, the effect of a rapidly changing milieu upon some
educators has been marked. The philosophies of James, Dewey,
and Whitehead have stirred their thinking and their practice.
Mackenzie, Forkner, and Corey draw some significant conclusions.[8] They call attention to the growing importance of work

[7] Maritain, *op. cit.*, p. 38.
[8] These appear in *The American High School: Its Responsibility and
Opportunity*, Eighth Yearbook of the John Dewey Society, New York,
Harper & Brothers, 1946.

experience, the necessity of giving work preparation in the high
school, the necessity for teaching subject matter that can be put
to use, the danger of wasting time on the policing of learning,
the tragedy of acquiring unwholesome learnings:

The orientation of a large proportion of the high school students
toward the professions has made it difficult to give serious and specific
attention to occupational choices on the high school level. The decision having been made early by parents of students in favor of a
profession and college training, careful consideration of frequently
more appropriate alternatives becomes quite impossible. It is estimated
that *six times as many high school students are admitted* to the college
preparatory course as actually finish college work. The many disappointments result in serious criticism of secondary education. Those
who look toward the professions but do not arrive are inclined to
blame the school for not aiding them to prepare for their vocational
fate. The New York State Regents' Inquiry and the American Youth
Commission studies reveal that only a small proportion of the high
school youth had vocational guidance, let alone vocational training.
The increasingly favorable economic position of the skilled worker
has attracted some attention away from white-collar jobs. Students
who eventually find a place in the trades, as well as those doing work
requiring little skill or special knowledge, feel, however, that the
school should have aided them in making a favorable vocational
adjustment. (The high schools enroll an increasing number destined
to be employed in distributive service and unskilled occupations.
Many will work at assembly-line tasks. The period of specific training
for most of these occupations is short.)

It has been proposed that many general problems in respect to
vocational orientation and preparation be given attention in the
school program. These include, for example, work habits, techniques
of getting along with people, and responsibilities with regard to labor
organizations and the welfare of the total social group. At the present
time, programs of work experience are being advocated because of
their potential contribution to occupational orientation, to common
occupational understandings, to the development of good work habits,
and to improve personal and social effectiveness.

Business has come to take a place beside labor in supporting education, and both look to its occupational values. Parents, too, give more and more thought to this outcome, especially when economic conditions are bad. Choosing and preparing for an occupation is one of the important developmental tasks of the adolescent. Still, educators have resisted a move in the direction of serious and careful preparation of students for a vocation in the high school. The academic orientation of teachers and administrators has undoubtedly prevented them from fully appreciating the occupational needs of youth not going on to college.

What is the responsibility of the high school in the vocational area? What program modifications, if any, should be made? [Gordon N. Mackenzie, on page 10.]

The common answer of withholding preparation for vocational adjustment until late in high school, or until after high school, as a solution to the labor supply problem also fails to take into account the interests of youth. Unless youth feels that school is worthwhile and unless the education they are getting is directly tied to after-school-life goals, they *may drop school* altogether. The recent survey of the educational levels of the boys in the army, who represent the cream of America's young manhood, shows that if vocational preparation is deferred to the last year of high school and beyond, the schools will fail to give approximately 60 percent of the young men the kind of education which will fit them best for vocational adjustment. The figures show, for example, that 31 percent of the men in the armed services never got as far as high school. Thirty percent more succeeded in getting into high school, but failed to stay until completion. Only 39 percent completed four years of high school, and only 3.6 percent completed four years of college or more. The number of men in the army who completed college is only one-tenth of one percent more than the number of men accepted into the army with four years of schooling or less. . . .

America must make certain not only that every boy and girl has a school available to him but also that the school program is one from which he will profit. America must face the challenge that if any boy or girl cannot attend school because of financial reasons, he or his family shall be subsidized for what he would earn if he were to drop school before he reached his capacity for participating fully in the economic, social, and political life of the nation. America subsidizes states for roads, pest control, flood control, soil and forest conservation. *Is it not reasonable to subsidize individuals for human conservation? . . .*

When every community has aggressively attacked the problem of preparing young people for the work of the world to the extent that every person feels his responsibility for doing his part of that work, we shall have gone a long way toward overcoming the threats to the American way. *When every individual feels he has a job to do and is prepared to do that job, and an opportunity for doing it is given him, we shall have built a rampart to strengthen the American way and the democratic way which will need no interior guard.* (Hamden L. Forkner, on page 180).

There are a number of serious consequences when the lessons suggested by high school teachers are unrelated, at least in a sensible and rational way in the judgment of the adolescent, to the problem that he is facing. The first of these consequences is that *what the adolescent "learns" under such circumstances is forgotten quickly for the simple and sufficient reason that it is not used.* This is made abundantly clear to anyone who cares to look into the research data on the retention of high school learning. Those facts and names and dates and principles and generalizations which are not used by adolescents as they wrestle with their developmental tasks are forgotten with a rapidity most disillusioning to those of us who feel that we can force boys and girls to learn things of no concern to them.

A second unfortunate consequence of our insistence that a great deal of time be spent by adolescents in high school engaging in learnings which make little or no difference to them is that we teachers and administrators must spend a great deal of our time *policing this learning.* If a girl learns general science in high school only because she realizes that she must learn general science in order to stay in high school with boys and girls whom she likes, the high school must make many provisions for policing her learning. If this is not done, the young lady will take advantage of the fact that she is already with boys and girls whom she likes and will proceed immediately to enjoy their company without going through the bothersome procedure of learning biology.

It is impossible to say what fraction of the nervous and physical energy of teachers is consumed by policing the learning of high school boys and girls in this sense, but the fraction certainly must be large. This policing is reduced somewhat by every step that modifies the high school curriculum in the direction of making it more significant and appropriate to the problems which are important to adolescents.

A third unfortunate consequence of school experiences which are not related to the concerns of adolescents is that while the boys and girls may, in order to attain real wants, complete the assignments, they also acquire concomitant learnings which are unwholesome. A fourteen-year-old boy with an I.Q. of 95 may force himself to read Byron's "Destruction of Sennacherib" and write an essay on it because he wants to stay in school or play football or to be eligible for a class office; but in all likelihood he will also learn never to read Byron again if he can help it, to avoid "good literature" in general, and to want to quit school as soon as he can. (Stephen M. Corey, on page 97.)

THE DISPOSITION OF THE CAPITAL OF HUMAN EXPERIENCE

Another educational problem has been the allocation of appropriate relative values to the psychological development of the individual and—along with it—the inculcation of subject matter. What shall be the centers of interest? To what extent shall they be vocational? Newton Edwards and Herman C. Richey, in their book, *The School in the American Social Order*, deal with these questions:

Even the most ardent champion of the traditional organization of knowledge cannot defend the way knowledge has been fractionalized and splintered by the multiplication of subjects and courses. All are agreed on the need for greater integration, for large configurations of meaning, for seeing more clearly the interrelationship between the various existing classifications of knowledge. It is not impossible that the historic classifications of knowledge are outmoded as the most effective carriers of human experience. And yet, if school subjects are to be abandoned and departmental lines in colleges and universities effaced, some centers of orientation must be devised to take their place. Certainly the student cannot be expected to attack the whole continent of knowledge simultaneously on all fronts and subdue it in one grand effort. We should not permit the recoil from overspecialization to throw us into confusion. It is a fair question to ask, just what are those about who propose the abandonment rather than the reorganization of subjects and departments? What new orientations do they propose: The problems of children and youth, the metaphysics of the great books, the major functions of social life? . . .

The scientific study of education has been oriented far too much around the concept of education as psychological process and far too little around the concept of education as public and social policy. . . .

Be they psychologists, psychiatrists, or philosophers, they tend to center attention on such matters as mental processes, individual differences, the development of personality, the interests and "felt" needs of children, the whole child, the role of experience in education, the cultivation of intellect, frustration and anxiety, developmental tasks of children, the peer culture, or the acculturation of the child in terms of social class. Certainly these are important matters with which we should be concerned but one should not be so preoccupied with them that in actual practice we accord little value to the concept of education as social engineering, as preparation for policy formation at the societal level. . . .

The two other current emphases also tend to deploy young people from the kind of education most essential to give them an understanding of the society of their own day. One of these is the insistence that a good education consists, in the main, of the cultivation of intellect and understanding of the great books; and the other, closely related, insists upon a return to the religious and classical traditions in education.[9]

GENERAL EDUCATION, THE CORE CURRICULUM,
COMMON LEARNINGS

As is clear from the foregoing discussion, the knowing or nondoing type of education has been justified, at various times, for all levels of society, at first for the patrician and later for the

[9] Newton Edwards and Herman C. Richey, *The School in the American Social Order*, Boston, Houghton Mifflin Company, 1947, pp. 854, 859, and 860.

plebeian. It has been concentrated in the "core curriculum" and in "common learnings." It attempts to *teach* more effectively those phases of everyday life which the pupil should learn to *live* more effectively. This is a worthy device, but in practice it is likely to block out the worthy, useful, vocational phases of education. What *is* a core curriculum of common learnings? One of our critics says it is what any person thinks he can teach best. Thus the persistent differences of opinion between schoolmen brought up in the academic tradition and the others of the vocational tradition.

Some definitions and distinctions follow:

The term *core* means the central part of the curriculum which is taken by every student. There are educational needs common to all children. The core program is designed to meet them.

What are these common needs in school education? In terms of the functional structure of an educational program, they may be defined as (1) social relationships, which are the subject matter; (2) English, which is an important medium of approach; (3) science, which is the method used; (4) the democratic way of life, which is the general purpose. If these be common needs of children in school-work, then the core program will be concerned chiefly with interests, methods, and objectives.[10]

There is no competition between general education and vocational education, or the common learnings and the differential learnings. They are both important. The time needed for common learnings is ever longer. Specialized education should immediately precede its need and use by the individual. General education should provide not only an adequate background against which an intelligent selection of a vocation can be made, but also the sense of direction and values against which a vocation can be truly evaluated.

Less than 20 percent of employed adults are employed in occupations of a professional and technical nature that require extended periods of collegiate and university training. Not more than 20 percent are engaged in the skilled and semi-skilled occupations that call for fairly extensive or expensive periods of training during the senior high school and junior college years. The majority are engaged in

[10] MacConnel, Miller, and Brandt, *Schools for a New Culture.*

occupational pursuits that place a premium on general competency, but in which specific skills are learned on the job.

These facts point to several questions:

(1) Is not a sound general education the best preparation for occupational life for the majority of youth?

(2) May not the securing of proficiencies in work experiences be the most promising avenue of occupational adjustment for well over 50 percent of youth?

(3) Would it not be best to limit vocational training for the skilled occupations to the 11th to 14th years of the secondary school?

(4) Despite its shortcomings, is not the comprehensive or cosmopolitan high school the most promising type of secondary school in the matter of providing programs which meet these differences in aptitude, interest, ability, and need?[11]

What is general education? General education is *general* in at least three respects:

First, general education is intended for everyone—not merely for the select few who become scholars or who enter the professions. No longer will preparation for college dominate the curriculum of the high school which is committed to the objectives of general education. The program of such a school will be planned to meet the varied needs of all of the young people of the community which it serves.

Second, general education is concerned with the total personality—not merely with the intellect but with emotions, habits, attitudes. General education regards the student as a single unified being rather than a compartment of knowledge, one of feelings and another of beliefs. This means that specific general education programs must be defined in terms of what the learner is or does rather than in terms of course content or a body of knowledge.

Third, general education is concerned with the individual's non-specialized activities. It consists of preparation for efficient living, no matter what one's vocation. This does not at all imply a lack of concern for vocational training. Since two of the responsibilities of every person are a contribution to society and the earning of his own living, general education should include the choosing of a vocation

[11] Galen Jones, *Teachers College Record*, April, 1949.

in relation to one's aptitudes and interests and to the needs of society. . . .

The hold of the academic tradition on the teachers and parents—and frequently children—constitutes a second major obstacle in the universalization of secondary education. As every informed teacher knows, there are almost innumerable improvements which could be made in the guiding and instructing of youth, to which no powerfully organized economic, political, patriotic, religious, or other level stands opposed. Yet secondary schools characteristically typify relatively few of these possible improvements—and more especially does this seem to be true of those which run afoul of the academic or "book learning" tradition. There can be no doubt but that the educators' failure to break with this tradition, at least for that preponderant majority of youth who do not plan to go to college, leads a great many youth to withdraw from secondary school.[12]

LIFE ADJUSTMENT

The Life Adjustment Commission has made valuable progress in approaching the needs of young people whose needs are not met by strictly college preparatory high schools and by the conventional vocational high schools. Good will and intentions characterize the efforts to arrive at a satisfactory solution. However, the testimony often seems heavily weighted on the "general" side. The following emphasizes the teaching of "general strengths." How does one *teach* "general strengths," and who is interested?

It is vital to the public welfare that all American youth can be educated for the common activities of life. Among the many common needs of all American youth are these:

1. To maintain health, even though they live where good health is not easily achieved.
2. To establish and maintain good homes, even though many forces draw their interests from their homes.

[12] Carey, Everett, and others, *General Education in the American High School*, Chicago, Scott, Foresman & Company, 1942, pp. 12 and 22.

3. To be co-operative in their relationships with employers and fellow workers and to be dependable in their jobs.

4. To understand activities and issues in their communities and in the world so that they can act intelligently, even though the issues they face are numerous and complicated.

5. To read, to write, to speak, to listen effectively.

6. To use leisure time profitably so that it becomes a cultural resource rather than a social liability.

It is *not* possible for the public high schools to provide the majority of youth with specific vocational training. The specific skills of most occupations can be learned only on the job.

It *is* possible for the public high schools to provide the majority with an education for resourcefulness and flexibility in many occupations. The schools are ideally suited as training grounds for developing certain general strengths which will equip all youth to meet their common daily needs.

Because high-school pupils bound for colleges and the skilled occupations have definite purposes, they often acquire these general strengths as by-products of their efforts to attain occupational competence. But they would benefit even more from direct training of these general strengths. For the majority such direct teaching has become an absolute necessity.[13]

PUSHING UP THE AGE FOR VOCATIONAL EDUCATION

The emphasis upon general education and common learnings inevitably implies the pushing up of the age for vocational instruction, thus postponing and, to a certain extent, nullifying the interest evoked by "doing" and vocation. However, here are two of the more understanding views, realizations of the importance of not drawing hard and fast lines between vocational and general education. Nevertheless, the tendency is to accept more "general" education during the high school years, even though the "doing" phases of vocational education are conceded to be of greatest importance. Note the final paragraph in the excerpt (below) from

[13] J. Dan Hull, *A Primer of Life Adjustment Education*, Chicago, American Technical Society, 1949.

Harl R. Douglass in which it is stated that "much of the specific vocational education will tend to be placed in the upper years beyond what is now the end of secondary education."

The statement of Harold Spears should be set over against what Douglass says. According to Spears, "It is not a true distinction to say that the core of general education trains for participation in social affairs, while vocational training more selfishly prepares the individual for an occupation. Social inter-action is as much a part of one's vocational existence as it is of one's avocational existence."

As a matter of fact, the greatest educational benefits are probably derived from specificity, precision, and responsibility in an established occupation, rather than from diffused generality. The next following quotation is from Spears:

Vocational education represents something more than general education—special education aimed at the perfection of the individual's power in respect to an occupation.

The two concepts of secondary education need not be competitive. With a reorganized social and economic order holding youth out of positions until at least eighteen years of age, vocational education is naturally being pushed to the eleventh and twelfth, or preferably to the thirteenth and fourteenth years of school, and in turn general education has an opportunity to grow up into the ninth, tenth, eleventh, and even twelfth years.

Out of a good general program will come the proper guidance into the vocational.

It is not a true distinction to say that the core of general education trains for participation in social affairs, while vocational training more selfishly prepares the individual for an occupation. Social interaction is as much a part of one's vocational existence as it is of his avocational existence.

If educational thought were justified in still holding faith in the acquisition of a certain group of cultural bodies of subject matter as preparation for proper participation in the present culture, then the curriculum problem could be solved by giving this common general core in the early secondary-school years, cutting it off abruptly as having been "acquired" and then polishing off the student in the upper years with his vocational training. The distinction will never be that sharp.

The new curriculum does not propose to select from the stock on hand those offerings which it reasons must be good for all pupils and then to mark them as the courses required of all pupils. To say health, recreation, English expression, safety, and a few others compose the common experiences in which all people are likely to engage is to endorse the procedure that school systems and state legislatures have been following for years in determining the high school curriculum. Any such area is broad, and if it is too heartily endorsed it will in itself act as a frame to hinder the provision of a suitable environment for the development of youth.[14]

Now let us consider the Douglass view:

For most youth, specific skills for a particular job are less important than work experience, attitudes toward work, and work habits. For example, a recent sampling study which covers 28 percent of the gainfully occupied population, believed to be representative of 70 percent of the American workers, reveals that more than two-thirds of the jobs demand of the workers who perform them successfully nothing beyond graduation from an elementary school. This argues that specific trade training, while of undoubted value for a few youth, is not the answer for the vast majority of youth. What they need is work experience, vocational guidance, placement, and an understanding of vocations and their possibilities. The argument that work experience habits and attitudes are more important than specific skills gains force when one considers the amount of training necessary to perform these tasks.

Employers stated that two-thirds of the workers assigned to jobs could reach full production in a week or less and that only 10 percent required more than six months or more of on-the-job training. Clearly, the school has a restricted responsibility in the field of intensive and specialized training for specific occupations. One must differentiate carefully, however, between vocational training for a

[14] Harold Spears, *The Emerging High School Curriculum*, New York, American Book Company, 1940, p. 68.

specific occupation and vocational education. The former is intensive concentration for a single occupation; the latter is devoted to occupational orientation and versatility. As such, it is part of general education—an inescapable responsibility of all schools seriously interested in preparing youth to meet the problems which they inevitably face in adult life.

Certain technical skills or highly skilled occupations require relatively long periods of training. An expert stenographer requires a considerable training period. The training of a tool or die maker is a long and arduous process which may be begun in a secondary school and continued for years in industry as an apprentice. For the highly skilled occupations, such as repairmen on dynamos, skilled mechanics to repair gasoline or diesel engines, and the professions, relatively long periods of preparation either in secondary schools and higher institutions or in industry supplemented by the schools is imperative. But data at hand indicate that only slightly more than 6 percent of our gainfully employed workers are engaged in the professions and that only one-eighth are engaged as foremen or skilled workers. About one-sixth are engaged in clerical occupations, but in no sense can all of them be classified as skilled workers. *For nearly half of the young people in the United States there is no alternative but employment as unskilled or semi-skilled laborers.* Both potential skilled workers and professional workers, as well as semi-skilled or unskilled laborers, need work experience as part of the educative process. In addition, skilled workers need further training secured in the secondary schools, in industry, or in higher institutions.

Certainly it may be argued that the school has a limited responsibility to furnish work experience, since the skills necessary on most jobs can be learned in a week or less. But the young person must know how to work, for a recent survey of 4,740 occupations in 40 industries indicated that two-thirds of the employers demanded at least some work experience as a prerequisite for initial employment.

The experience of the 1930's has indicated clearly that work is necessary in maintaining self-respect both for adults and youth. In order to achieve adult status in society, it is necessary to hold a job for which pay is given, or to believe that one has the ability to get and hold a job. Learning how to work is helpful in getting a job; getting a job is the first big hurdle in economic independence and adult status. It is one of the "developmental tasks" which all young people face.

The actual transition from school to work will probably advance to a point somewhere in the neighborhood of 20 years of age for most young people. As this development occurs, it is logical that more time in the early secondary years should be devoted to general education and that much of the specific vocational education will tend to be placed in the upper years beyond what is now the end of secondary education for the majority of pupils.[15]

"IMPERATIVE NEED NO. 1"

The pressing need for a more alert system of vocational education is borne out by the National Association of Secondary School Principals (who, with few exceptions, are principals of academic high schools) in a bulletin called *Planning for American Youth*, published in 1944 and supplemented in 1949 with a check list on the original. As the editors say, "The Association has attempted in several ways to encourage American schools to *act* to meet the Imperative Needs of Youth. It is notable that Imperative Need No. 1 has been, 'All Youth need to develop saleable skills and those understandings and attributes that make the worker an intelligent and productive participant in economic life.'" Nine other needs are stated, but the vocational need is No. 1.

"EDUCATION FOR *All* AMERICAN YOUTH"

In 1944 the Educational Policies Commission published an exciting work with this title. Again a body not primarily vocational, but appointed by the National Education Association of the United States and the American Association of School Administrators, placed "Preparation for Occupations" as the first area of learning for youth and assigned to it increasing allotments of time from the 10th to the 14th year.

[15] Harl R. Douglass, *The High School Curriculum*, New York, The Ronald Press Company, 1947, pp. 274 and 297.

While this proposal meets only in part the needs and purposes set up by the present study, it does demand a flexibility of curriculum which, if it included industrial arts and were stretched to its ultimate limits, could adequately provide a well-rounded general and vocational education for all youth. An outline of the Commission's program will be given in Chapter V for comparison with actual, going programs in existing schools.

THE RELATION OF INDUSTRIAL ARTS TO VOCATIONAL EDUCATION

Among educators, and especially among teachers of industrial arts and of vocational education, there is considerable understanding of the differences involved in teaching these two types of manual work. Industrial arts imparts general *information* about industry, teaches simple manipulation, develops aesthetic appreciation, is avocational, and provides vocational guidance. Vocational education imparts varying degrees of skill, is on a strictly trade basis, and prepares for a job. Industrial arts has a definite place in education, but should not be confused with vocational education, with which this study is concerned. The following quotations will clarify the purpose of industrial arts:

Industrial arts activities may, to some extent, contribute to the meeting of certain needs of children in the economic-vocational field. A child or a youth has a basic feeling that he is growing toward a position of economic independence and a place in the vocational scheme of things. An industrial arts program provides try-out opportunities where some of the important occupational fields may be sampled. While no attempt is made in industrial arts classes to provide vocational skills, the child is nevertheless impressed by the fact that he is using the tools and processes of industry and that he is being given the opportunity to study and select from the trades and occupations of adult society. . . .

Important objectives in industrial arts are:

1. To explore industry and American industrial civilization in terms of its organization, raw materials, processes and operations, products, and occupations.

2. To develop recreational and avocational activities in the area of constructive work.

3. To increase an appreciation for good craftsmanship and design, both in the products of modern industry and in artifacts from the material cultures of the past.

4. To increase consumer knowledges to a point where students can select, buy, use, and maintain the products of industry intelligently.

5. To provide information about, and—insofar as possible—experiences in, the basic processes of many industries, in order that students may be more competent to choose a future vocation.

6. To encourage creative expression in terms of industrial materials.

7. To develop desirable social relationships, such as cooperation, tolerance, leadership and fellowship, and tact.

8. To develop a certain amount of skill in a number of basic industrial processes.[16]

COLLEGE ENTRANCE REQUIREMENTS

How to achieve a flexible curriculum? This study is not primarily concerned with the objectives of American colleges or with their curricula. However, it *is* concerned with the manner in which college entrance requirements affect secondary school curricula. Several facts are notable:

1. Secondary school curricula (except for those in vocational high schools) have been determined largely by the demands of the colleges.

2. During the last fifty years there has been considerable diversification of offerings in some colleges and therefore some easing in requirements, but the pattern is still there.

3. A few voices have been raised in support of the thesis that intensive work in any secondary field is good preparation for college. On the same basis there is usually a demand that those students who want to pursue an academic program in

[16] Gordon O. Wilber, *Industrial Arts in Vocational Education,* Scranton, International Text Book Company, 1948, pp. 27 and 42.

college should prove their ability in the same kind of program in high school.

4. The problem leads ultimately to the question, Who should go to what kind of colleges? As Ordway Tead queries, "Are not the aims of the most academic colleges subtly vocational?" (His views are cited on a later page.)

5. For this study, the question is, What should be taught in the secondary school so as to offer the optimum of culture and vocational education to *all* American youth?

THE MICHIGAN SECONDARY SCHOOL-COLLEGE AGREEMENT

One of the most hopeful signs of improved relations between high schools and colleges lies in the Michigan Agreement, which has resulted from the Michigan Study of the Secondary School Curriculum launched in 1937. A major obstacle to change in the traditional pattern of secondary school offerings was found to be the problem of college entrance requirements. "To what extent this was a real or simply a psychological barrier is perhaps a moot question. Nevertheless, college entrance requirements were frequently cited as reasons why a given high school could not make certain changes in its program which it regarded as desirable."[17]

The result of the Michigan Study was an Agreement, which was in operation from 1940 to 1950, and has recently been revised and established as a continuing relationship. The principal sections are as follows:

1. It is proposed that this Agreement be extended to include any accredited high school whose staff will make the commitments noted below in Section Two. The Agreement is as follows: "The college agrees to disregard the pattern of subjects pursued in considering

[17] This quotation and other material relating to the Agreement are excerpted from an article about it by Leon S. Waskin in the *Bulletin of the National Association of Secondary-School Principals*, January, 1949.

for admission the graduates of selected accredited high schools, provided they are recommended by the school from among the more able students in the graduating class. This Agreement does not imply that students must be admitted to certain college courses or curricula for which they cannot give evidence of adequate preparation."

Secondary schools are urged to make available such basic courses as provide a necessary preparation for entering technical, industrial, or professional curricula. It is recommended further that colleges provide accelerated programs of preparation for specialized college curricula for those graduates who are unable to secure such preparatory training in high school.

2. High schools which seek to be governed by this Agreement shall assume responsibility for and shall furnish evidence that they are initiating and continuing such procedures as the following:

a. A program involving the building of an adequate personal file about each student, including testing data of various kinds, anecdotal records, personality inventories, achievement samples, etc. The high-school staff will assume responsibility for developing a summary of these personnel data for submission to the college.

b. A basic curriculum study and evaluation of the purposes and program of the secondary school.

c. Procedures for continuous follow-up of former pupils.

d. A continuous program of information and orientation throughout the high-school course regarding the nature and requirements of certain occupations and specialized college courses. During the senior year, to devote special emphasis to the occupation or college of the pupil's choice.

3. It is understood that high schools which cannot or will not make and observe the above commitments (See Section Two) will continue to employ the major and minor sequences for those students who wish to attend college.[18]

The stimulation given by the Agreement to secondary curriculum experimentation in many areas has been highly encouraging. The principals of the Midland High School and the Redford Union High School, commenting on the importance of judging

[18] From the mimeographed text of the Agreement as approved by the Michigan College Association and the Michigan Secondary-School Association.

a student's prospects on the basis of excellence in vocational subjects, are quoted (respectively) as follows:

To the larger high school there is one big advantage that we have made use of and will continue to do so. We find that one or two percent of our students each year find that the financial status of the family has suddenly changed for the better and it is possible for this student to attend college. Previously, the student had *taken some kind of a vocational course* to prepare himself for job opportunities on leaving high school. If this student in question is one of college caliber as far as ability is concerned, we now have a way of enrolling him in a college.

About two years ago I had the question of college entrance brought to my attention in a very clear way. I had a student who ranked fourth in a class of 103 and desired to be a social science teacher. I recommended her for a state teacher training college where she was refused, although she had 190 hours credit. She had sequences in commercial, English, social science, and homemaking. They replied that, if our high school were acceptable to the College Agreement Committee, they would accept her. A year later we were accepted, but a good candidate had been lost to the teaching profession.

Waskin concludes his article by saying:

These descriptions contain ample evidence that the Secondary School-College Agreement in Michigan has provided the stimulus for a great many promising activities at the local level that, in the aggregate, point toward the general improvement of instruction in secondary schools throughout the state. It is in this facilitation of the development of functional local programs that the principal significance of the Secondary School-College Agreement lies rather than in the fact that it provides an alternate method for securing admission to college. At the same time, any school that assumes seriously its obligations under the Agreement will be in the position of providing each college with far more comprehensive and significant information about each applicant than has been customary in the past. Furthermore, the whole program provides a clear demonstration of the fact that the relinquishing of the untenable assumption that any college or any state educational authority knows exactly what is best for each high school need not result in chaos nor in frustrated, helpless fumbling by the local school. Here is one way of both releasing and harnessing the energies of local communities in a cooperative attack upon the numerous and difficult problems of developing a truly democratic educational program in our American democratic society.

A SURVEY REPORT ON COLLEGE ENTRANCE REQUIREMENTS

The best research study of entrance requirements is that of Benjamin Fine. Here is his summary of the latest trends, along with conclusions and recommendations:

What Type of High School Program Is Best?

How important are the college preparatory courses for the student? Is there a significant correlation between the type of program taken by the student in high school and his work in college? *The overwhelming majority of the colleges—all but 10 or 15 percent— still cling tenaciously to the academic or classical programs.* Are they justified in doing so? The question of relaxing the type of high school program required for entering college has been argued and debated in academic circles for many years, without any definite conclusions. Even in the progressive schools' eight-year experiment, where the pattern of subjects was not considered to be of primary importance, the *students did take a minimum of the "solids"—languages, mathematics, history, science, English.* Are these subjects necessary for college success?

What High School Subject Is Best?

In a survey of "the type of high school curriculum which has the best preparation for college," J. A. Yates based his findings on the complete high school and college transcripts, including testing records, of 706 graduates of three universities—Cincinnati, Kentucky, and Indiana. Entrance credits were classified into four types of curricula: Classical, general, scientific, and vocational. *No significant differences could be found in the value of any high school curriculum for any particular curriculum or major in college.* Yates concluded: "The influence of the type of high school curriculum was negligible. The low correlations emphasize the importance of other factors involved which may be summed up in terms of teacher ability and pupil activity."

Vocational Subjects Valuable

In the bulletin of the Virginia Polytechnic Institute, Edmund C. Magell, in discussing the college performance of high school graduates of *a course in vocational agriculture as compared with others, declares that vocational agriculture serves fully as well in preparation for college despite the curriculum elected in college, as do the other high school courses which are replaced by agriculture—that is, languages and sometimes a third year of mathematics or history.* Dr. Magell continues: "There is no evidence that the traditional academic subjects either singly or in groups have any greater educational value for the individual either for life or for college preparation as compared with vocational and other subjects, and prescriptions in them for college entrance should be reduced to what can be justified. . . . Colleges are surprisingly slow to change entrance requirements even in view of the evidence; and they are themselves not doing enough research to develop and perfect improved methods of selecting students."

As a result of his study Dr. Magell recommended "that the idea of a college preparatory curriculum, at least for rural high schools, be eliminated, since all of the evidence to date disproves the assumption that there is any group of courses or individual courses which are superior for college preparation."

Conclusions

Several significant conclusions emerge:

1. Seventy-five percent of all the colleges in this country give preference to students who take the academic, classical or college preparatory course.

2. A vast majority of the colleges insist that students who desire to continue into college take work in English, algebra, geometry, foreign languages, social studies, and physical sciences.

3. Within the framework of a traditional program the colleges recommend that the student be given leeway to specialize in the subjects of his choice.

4. In addition to recommending the pattern or type of program

to be taken by the student, the college insists that the quality of the work be high.

5. No data exist to indicate which subject is "best" for the student, or which will predict success in college.

Recommendations

Despite the overwhelming response of the colleges of the country in favor of the traditionally academic program, I believe that the colleges should reexamine their attitudes and explore the possibilities of introducing a less rigid schedule. It is not altogether evident that a student who has taken a vocational or a commercial program will not be able to fit into the college life. Instead of asking for fifteen units, most of them in academic fields, the colleges should develop a flexible program and accept high school graduates regardless of the pattern of the course taken. This is the case to some extent in the state universities, especially in many of the midwestern and western states where by state regulation the universities are required to take all graduates of accredited high schools. Yet, even in those institutions, frequently the high school graduate must have a certain pattern of courses before he can enter; *it is doubtful, for example, if a state university would take a high school graduate if his courses were weighted with technical and vocational subjects.*

The following specific recommendations are offered for consideration by America's colleges and universities:

1. Entrance requirements should be modified to permit high school graduates who have not taken the regular academic course to enter.

2. Greater flexibility should be developed concerning the fifteen Carnegie units of admission now required throughout the land. Either these units should be discontinued and some more effective basis of admitting students adopted, or else *they should be altered so as to include such courses as vocational agriculture, shopwork, mechanical drawing, typewriting, and similar non-academic courses.*

3. A premium should not be put on students who have been able to master foreign languages, mathematics, or science in the high school. The general ability rather than type of program pursued by the candidate should be the ultimate criterion of his potential college ability.

4. Students who do not meet the requirements so far as high

school subjects are concerned should, if they otherwise show promise, be admitted to college on an equal basis with the other students.

If these recommendations were put into effect the colleges might be swamped with candidates for admittance, but that, in a democracy, is the goal—to get into college as many as possible of those who can benefit. By making the entrance requirements less rigid, the student body might be doubled in a decade. This would not necessarily mean "cheapening" the college degree; just as many intelligent students are kept out of college by the present system as are permitted to enter. It would mean broadening the college base.

A new philosophy is needed—calling for a policy of greater flexibility and less rigidity, and a more mature consideration of the individual differences of the boys and girls who are now attending high school.[19]

VOCATIONAL IMPLICATIONS IN COLLEGE EDUCATION

Despite the overwhelming practice of colleges in basing admission on proficiency in academic subjects, the curricula of the colleges themselves are, as pointed out below, subtly vocational. Ordway Tead's position as Chairman of the Board of Higher Education, directing all four New York City Colleges, enables him to make this claim with a considerable degree of authority:

It is not easy to make oneself understood when one flatly affirms that there should be a greater vocational focus for virtually all students in college education. Let us be honest and recognize that many college teachers who still profess the ideal of a liberal arts education without vocational contamination are, nevertheless, spending much of their time on what they know to be pre-medical, pre-law, pre-teaching, or pre-some-or-other vocational instruction. Indeed every effort of the teacher to induce his abler students into making an ultimate vocation of the subject which is his own major interest, is itself an unacknowledged vocational emphasis. . . .

. . . one of the most important springs of interest, one of the most sustaining motives to intellectual application, is the student's con-

[19] Benjamin Fine, *Admission to American Colleges*, New York, Harper & Brothers, 1946, pp. 97-100.

viction that this or that subject or course of study is qualifying him for a useful career.

Of course the college is not a glorified occupational placement office, it is certainly not to conduct its courses with a commercial utilitarian aim. But in our kind of society it is through work that all of us not only register in self-esteem and social acceptance, but it is in work that we find for the most part our creative challenge and our social contributions. What I am thus pleading for is that each college teacher must teach with a more than nominal awareness that somehow and by somebody the work of the world has to be done. And I suspect that if more college teachers could be induced to spend their three months' holiday at some work other than teaching, they might naturally come to a corrective in their basic outlook on the student's predicament. And this might go a long way in supplying the vocational focus which I am urging for adoption. In other words there is an important difference between a sympathetic and informed portrayal of vocational prospects and the offering of narrowly vocational subjects and courses. And I am pleading for the former, not the latter.[20]

"INTEREST" AND "DOING"

Probably the most effective type of procedure, in terms of child psychology, is that followed in the kindergarten. The children are so young and so active that it is only through an appeal to interest and an offering of activity that they can be kept in order for any kind of cooperative effort. However, from that point on there seems to be a gradual diminution of interest and activity in favor of traditional educational and social demands. All this despite the growing conviction that "there is no learning without interest and that we learn only what we do." The role of vocational education is obviously of the greatest importance.

At least one of the reasons for this submission to tradition,

[20] Ordway Tead, in an address at the National Conference on Higher Education, Chicago, April 4, 1949. Printed in *College and University*, July 1949.

which has been called the "condensed originality of a people," is given in the following words:

Perhaps New-Fist, the Paleolithic founder of formal education, planned a new curriculum on a clean page. But that legendary character is the only schoolman who ever had that opportunity. Since his time, every educator desiring to change the curriculum has found that he has had to deal with pupils who knew what their predecessors had been taught, teachers who were satisfied with what they had been doing, and parents whose desires for their children's education were based upon approval of, or protest against, their own education.[21]

[21] Giles, McCutcheon, and Zechiel, *Adventure in American Education*, Vol. II, "Exploring the Curriculum," New York, Harper & Brothers, 1942, p. 70.

V. What Do Our High Schools Teach?

A contrast in courses

How do curricula of academic and vocational high schools compare? The educational theories which we have discussed have had some testing in actual curricular experimentation.

We here submit significant findings from a survey of secondary curricula in 71 cities in 42 states and the District of Columbia. Both general and vocational high schools are represented.[1] We consider the "academic" content of vocational school curricula and the "vocational" content of general high school curricula. We pay special attention to the courses offered and the requirements for graduation in 19 high schools of the general type, while vocational schools are viewed from the standpoint of college preparation. We compare the usual schedule of semester periods in a general high school with the schedule in several vocational schools. Student manuals and other orientation material furnished to students for their guidance provided the data utilized for purposes of curriculum analysis. In addition, we obtained information regarding the entrance requirements of 43 state universities, to determine how many units of credit toward admission were granted for vocational courses taken in high school.

Conclusions from the data presented in Appendices 3, 4, and 5 are subject to certain limitations. A few states (Florida, Iowa,

[1] Typical vocational high schools have also been described by Kahler and Hamburger in *Education for an Industrial Age*, quoted in Chapter IX.

Nebraska, North Carolina, Vermont, and Wyoming) are absent from the list of schools, though probably without any great effect on the general picture. No rural schools are included, and the picture therefore relates to the urban, and larger, high schools of the nation. It should be borne in mind, too, that all of the schools encompassed in the survey greatly exceed the medians for both pupil registration and number of faculty members in the country as a whole. If these qualifications be taken into account, we believe that the findings of the study have undoubted significance and value within its properly understood intention and scope. The importance of vocational education in rural schools is recognized at the end of this chapter and in other chapters.

A NATIONAL PATTERN DISCLOSED

1. *Units Required for Graduation.* In the main there is a general standard throughout the country in the total number of units, credits, or points required for high school graduation, i.e., 16 units or 32 credits for the four-year course, and 12 units for the three-year course. This is what is required in New York City, with the addition there of two units which are given for the required work in health education, music, and art. Although health education is required in all of the schools which were studied, few of them require either art or music. In those instances where more than 16 units are required, we find that health education and physical education are granted from one to three units of credit.

These unit requirements for graduation are in the main a reflection of college entrance requirements, which are standardized insofar as the number of units (15) for admission are concerned.

A query in terms of the evaluation of a high school education may be raised at this point. Should all high school students, regardless of the course which they are pursuing, be required to complete the same number of units? Essentially, units of credit may be translated into units of time because, with the exception of courses in typewriting, health education, some courses in music, and the three-hour "Smith-Hughes" shop courses, all subjects carry the same credit.

2. *Subjects Required for Graduation.* Here, too, a fairly consistent pattern obtains. All of the high schools require at least three years of English (including the one year in the ninth grade of junior high school), one year of American history, and three to four years of physical education.

Beyond these three courses, we find variation in the other specific subject requirements. A minimum of one year in both mathematics and science is a further requirement in most of the schools. The grouping of courses into major and minor sequences of three and two units, respectively, is also usually required. The general policy is to require one major sequence in addition to the English with two minor sequences.

Three schools—the Holyoke High School in Holyoke, Massachusetts; the Joliet Township High School in Joliet, Illinois; and the Senior High School in Springfield, Missouri—require that all pupils take one year of industrial arts or homemaking, or, in the case of the Springfield School, some other handwork course.

3. *Electives.* Of the sixteen units required for graduation, approximately only eight are specified, English, social studies, mathematics, and science. The eight remaining units are electives. The opportunities for election are in most instances limited by the pupil's choice of a curriculum, with the greatest degree of limitation for those pupils enrolled in the college preparatory curriculum, in which additional units in mathematics, science, and foreign language are specified. The pupils with the greatest freedom in the election of subjects are the industrial arts and general course majors.

Aside from the selection of their major vocational course,

pupils in the vocational high schools have little or no choice in the selection of the nonvocational courses. The curriculum is rather well fixed with some variations in the related subject area, i.e., science, mathematics, and drawing, depending upon the vocation in which the pupil is enrolled.

4. *Comparative Loads of Pupils in Several High Schools and Those in Vocational Schools.* In contrast to the usual 25- to 30-period program that a pupil carries in the general high school, the established period schedule in the vocational high schools represents an increased load ranging from 33⅓ to 40 percent. The vocational high school pupil may be represented as taking the same program as his contemporary in an industrial arts course in a general high school, plus 15 additional periods of shop work. This is seen by contrasting the schedules for pupils enrolled in college preparatory and industrial arts courses in a general high school with those pupils enrolled in straight vocational courses and combined vocational and college preparatory courses in a vocational high school (see Appendix 2).

The college preparatory course in a New York City general high school and the combined college preparatory and vocational course at Metropolitan Vocational High School in New York City for Grades 10, 11, and 12 may also be compared in terms of semester periods, with the same results apparent (see Appendix 3).

VOCATIONAL TRAINING IN THE ACADEMIC SCHOOLS

We offer a brief analysis of the curricula and requirements for graduation from 19 general high schools (see Appendix 4). These schools are representative of all the general high schools studied, and all offer the college preparatory course (which hence is not indicated on the chart). Shop courses are shown to demonstrate the varieties of vocational training experiences which students may elect. Contrasting these curricula with those of the vocational high schools previously shown, we see that in the vocational school the pattern ordinarily calls for 50 percent of the schedule (usually thirty clock hours a week) to be devoted to shop work and the other 50 percent to academic and related subjects (science, mathematics, drawing, etc.).

With few exceptions, all the general high schools studied provide courses in homemaking for girls and in industrial arts for boys. But beyond these basic courses, there is a wide range in the number and variety of opportunities for vocational training. Most of the schools offering vocational courses permit the pupils to take these for five periods a week. Usually, a unit of industrial arts is a prerequisite for further shop work. Some schools have their shop classes organized on a Smith-Hughes formula which allows the students to get 15 hours a week of training in a specific shop. However, in these instances, only one year of such training may be taken.

ACADEMIC TRAINING IN THE VOCATIONAL SCHOOLS

Among vocational and technical schools which prepare for college, nine outside of New York state that they train both for trade and higher education. These high schools are the Paul Hayne in Birmingham, Alabama; Gerstmeyer Technical in Terre Haute, Indiana; Cass Technical in Detroit, Michigan; Hadley Technical in St. Louis, Missouri; Bayonne Technical and Vocational in Bayonne, New Jersey; Derry County Vocational in Derry Township, Hershey, Pennsylvania; San Antonio Technical and Vocational in San Antonio, Texas; Boys Technical in Milwaukee, Wisconsin; and Williamsport Senior (technical-vocational course) in Williamsport, Pennsylvania.

With the exception of the Paul Hayne Vocational High School and the Williamsport Senior High School, these schools adhere to the Smith-Hughes formula in respect to time allotments for shop work and the related and academic subjects. Each of these

exceptions provides a combined vocational and college preparatory course. It does so by giving eight units of academic work in
the first two years in addition to a course in occupations and industrial relations. Shop work on a three-hour-per-day basis is
given in the third and fourth years with at least four additional
units in academic subjects. Williamsport does so by requiring a
longer school day, usually to the extent of two hours of evening
attendance a week.

Whether or not the Hadley Technical High School in St.
Louis, Missouri, may be classified as a vocational high school is
not clear, although it also follows the Smith-Hughes pattern. The
following statement of its aim shows that it is also a college
preparatory:

The primary function of this school is to provide educational
experiences for students who desire training for the purpose of
obtaining immediate, useful, and gainful employment. College entrance requirements may also be fulfilled if the student expresses
such a desire a year or more before his date of graduation.

In New York City 11 of the 31 vocational high schools are
now offering a technical course which is also college preparatory.
In these schools the program calls for 15 periods of shop work
and 25 periods of academic and technical subjects. At the Metropolitan Vocational High School a special academic program is
provided for pupils who wish to enter college or the maritime
academies. At this school pupils may carry four academic courses
plus a half day of shop. Pupils who begin their work in the
ninth year may earn a total of 25 high school units, one third
more than are required in the general high schools. Study of the
programs in the specialized high schools, such as the Bronx High
School of Science, the Brooklyn Technical High School, the
High School of Music and Art, the Stuyvesant High School, and
the vocational high schools mentioned above, shows that in all
these schools the pupils complete from three to six more units of

courses than are required of their contemporaries in the other schools. In effect, the pupils in the technical courses in the vocational high schools, in addition to obtaining fundamental trade training, are also completing the standard academic course given in a general high school.

DISTRIBUTIVE AND DIVERSIFIED OCCUPATIONS

Training opportunities in these fields are usually restricted to seniors. In addition to the "on the job training," for which two units of credit are granted, the pupils carry two other subjects, including one in vocational civics which is usually taught by the teacher who acts as coordinator between the school and the employer.

In practice this is similar to the cooperative program in some New York City general and vocational high schools. Pupils on the cooperative programs spend one week in school and one week on the job. This program is restricted to juniors and seniors in the general high schools and to seniors in the vocational schools.

THE SPLIT PROGRAM

In an interesting variant some schools offer a split program. Tacoma, Washington; Holyoke, Massachusetts; Denver, Colorado; and Salt Lake City, Utah, permit their high school seniors to spend half of the day in their home school and the other half in the city's vocational high school. They take two subjects in the home school and three hours of vocational work in the vocational high school.

LIBERALIZING THE LIBERAL ARTS

The entrance requirements to 43 state universities have also been studied. Of these, 28 grant from one to six credits for non-academic subjects such as shop work, agriculture, music, industrial art, homemaking, and commercial subjects. The average is approximately four credits for these subjects. Five—California, New Jersey (Rutgers), Penn State, Rhode Island, and Vermont—will accept none, and ten do not indicate the nonacademic subjects among those acceptable for admission. Twelve will accept as electives any courses which are accepted by an accredited high school for its diploma. Details of the study will be found in Appendix 5.

The private colleges and universities ordinarily specify academic subjects as the sole courses for which they will give credits. There are many exceptions to this rule, indicating that these institutions are developing an appreciation of the values in subject fields other than those traditionally designated as college preparatory.

The University of Illinois, a state university, takes note of such values in its catalogue, in which it states: "The University realizes the obligation of the high school to meet fully the needs and interests of all its pupils. It, therefore, believes that high schools should offer courses in such fields as agriculture, art, commerce, home economics, industrial arts, and music. Furthermore, by accepting them for admission, it recognizes that they contribute to satisfactory preparation for college work." The catalogue for the University of Georgia contains a similar statement. Further departure from the traditional imposition of entrance requirements by the colleges may be noted in another section of the Illinois catalogue: "The six remaining units necessary for admission may be selected from any of the high-school subjects which are accepted by an accredited school toward its diploma and which meet the standards for accrediting as defined by the University of Illinois." Similar statements appear in ten state university catalogues. Brooklyn College—a municipal institution in New York City's college system—permits applicants to present as many as three units in elective work from "any other subject(s) credited in a recognized high school."

Such liberalization of college entrance requirements may well affect the standard college preparatory course that most high school youth follow. It may be possible, therefore, for all high school youth to find that work experiences of different kinds are truly educational in that they can serve not only as an introduction to the realities of work but also as a means of getting into college.

The curricula for each school are classified according to the designation used by the school. In some instances, different designations may indicate the same source. The shop courses are listed in order to show the varieties of vocational training experiences which pupils may elect.

VARIATIONS IN STANDARDIZATION

The telescopic view afforded by this curricular survey in the high schools of the larger American communities indicates the degree to which our schools have conformed with the pattern imposed upon them by the colleges. The variations taking place in the formerly rigid courses of study are, in the main, the results of a changing student body, which today represents a cross section of our youth, in marked contrast to the selective high school enrollment of fifty years ago, and as affected by the impact of industry and commerce and the dynamics of our social order. These forces, among others, have caused the schools to loosen the constrictive bindings of college entrance requirements. Although 16 units are still the open sesame to a high school diploma, the nature of the units has changed. New courses have been introduced in attempts to meet the needs of the larger number who are not college bound; and for those going on to higher education, a richer variety of subject matter is now available.

RURAL SCHOOLS IN THE UNITED STATES

As already noted, this study does not include rural schools. In discussion of secondary school curricula it is a common error to neglect consideration of the difficulties encountered by small rural schools, of which there are many. Here are the pertinent facts, as given at the White House Conference on Rural Education, October, 1944.

On the high school level, too, smallness is the outstanding characteristic, one out of five attempting four years of high school work, with a staff of but one or two teachers, and three out of five with four teachers or fewer. . . .

Since parents insist that every high school must provide an open door to the college, these factors compel the small school to devise special procedures or to limit its offerings to college preparation, despite the fact that few of its products will aspire to this level of education. . . .

Three means of meeting this situation are:

1. Correspondence courses.
2. Circuit teachers (joint employment of specialists by two or more small schools).
3. Consolidation.

Since half the young men born on farms will have to find jobs elsewhere and rural children need guidance to solve educational and vocational difficulties, which the rural environment often imposes, use of guidance specialists on a regional or county basis is desirable. . . .

Rural is defined as open country and all villages and homes up to 2500 population (census definition). . . .

In 1938, of 16,000,000 rural children between 5 and 17 years of age 12,000,000 enrolled in rural schools.

These figures are very close to those for cities, the urban child population being slightly less than the rural and the urban population slightly more.

Further details on rural schools are given in Works and Lesser:[2]

The rural high school in particular, must be concerned with preparing its students for work. Those of its students who intend to remain on the farm and those who migrate to cities both need vocational preparation. The boys and girls who are already assuming

[2] Works and Lesser, *Rural Education Today*, Chicago, University of Chicago Press, 1942, p. 131.

responsibility in connection with farm and home not only require instruction in the several disciplines involved in their work and impinging upon it, but would find their school work sterile and devoid of reality if it neglected the fields of interest around which their lives are already beginning to center. Students who will migrate to cities need vocational preparation so that they will not be handicapped in finding jobs and will be able to do productive work for which they are fitted. In the case of this group of students, too, there is a fortunate identity of interests and needs; several studies have shown that rural youth have a bent for mechanical and technical pursuits. Vocational preparation is winning a place in the rural school curriculum because it at once serves the needs and commands the interest of the majority of students—as many as ninety-seven in every one hundred in some schools—who must attempt to prepare themselves while in high school for homemaking and for earning a living.

The need for a broad, general program must include offerings in a number of difficult fields for purposes of exploratory experiences. Few rural schools can afford trade and industrial training. Following are examples of good programs.

The Ridgefield (Washington) High School offers its more mature students a pre-vocational course which covers elementary carpentry, gas engine operation; electricity, including wiring line work, and armature winding; tool room work and steel lathe operation. In addition to exploring and developing some skills in these fields, the boys study shop mathematics, personal budgets, insurance and taxes, and their rights and responsibilities as workers.

The Whitehaven School (Shelby County, Tennessee, near Memphis) has a comprehensive trade and industrial program which provides four years of training in any of the following fields: welding and sheet metal, woodworking, mechanical shop, drafting, electrical work, auto mechanics and painting. Students spend three hours a day throughout their high school careers in one vocational department. Much of their remaining work is in closely related fields, but the school insists on four years of English and offers a diversified curriculum. Whitehaven's program goes a long way toward paying its own way. The shops constitute a group of factories and a mechanical service organization for the rural schools of Shelby County.

VI. Cases in Point

Some typical double-purpose schools

In the preceding chapters is presented an overview of the curricula and the requirements for graduation in 19 United States high schools of the general type. We have also outlined the characteristic pattern for vocational schools. These data indicate that it is feasible to combine in one school adequate preparation for both entrance to an occupation and admission to college. The same conclusion can be drawn from a close examination of those schools where definite and specific attempt is already being made, with notable success, to meet both of these objectives.

Twelve such schools are now described from material furnished by them and checked by their respective principals. Eight of them have been administered or visited by various members of the Project staff. The following "stories" speak for themselves, as examples of what is now being done and of what could be done to supply educational needs by such means as are provided in these double-purpose schools.

THE METROPOLITAN VOCATIONAL HIGH SCHOOL,
NEW YORK CITY

Under the aegis of a single school organization, the Metropolitan Vocational High School serves the needs of a student body totaling 2,000 full-time vocational high school pupils and 1,000 part-time continuation-school pupils. In terms of I.Q. the range is from 60 to 160. This range of necessity requires a multiple-track academic schedule. Hence about one fourth of the pupils are successfully combining their vocational work with a college preparatory program. At the other extreme are about eighty pupils selected for special courses by the Bureau for Children with Retarded Mental Development. In between is the main part of the student body, following the typical vocational high school program of shop and related subjects.

The vocational courses are grouped in three major divisions: maritime occupations (deck, engine, radio, steward, boatbuilding, electrical), performing arts (dance, drama, music), and commercial photography. In addition the school offers barbering and hairdressing, beauty culture, and an exploratory course in printing. All courses, except for maritime and barbering, are for both boys and girls. And with the exception of printing, beauty culture, boatbuilding, music, and commercial photography, the special courses are offered in no other city high school.

There is good reason for this. Though the school of today bears little resemblance to its original, Metropolitan was in fact founded in 1920 as the East Side Continuation School, with an enrollment of 14,000 pupils who were required to attend one four-hour session a week. Some 15 years ago the school was faced with the fact that its neighborhood population was steadily decreasing. Further, with the school-leaving age raised to 16 and with depression years limiting the employment opportunities for all youth, the continuation-school enrollment dropped to 3,500. Concomitantly, the need for more full-time schools increased. This led to the introduction at East Side of a two-year industrial high school course, later to become Metropolitan's full four-year vocational high school program.

The traditional vocational courses—in auto mechanics, electrical wiring, woodworking, dressmaking, and so on—were readily available in other schools throughout the city. This situation presented the school with an opportunity to pioneer in occupations not being taught elsewhere. As the largest and most important port in the country, New York City was an ideal community in which to give courses in the maritime occupations. Metropolitan Vocational High School introduced those courses. Similarly, courses in the performing arts were a natural choice for the capital of the drama, dance, and music field.

Metropolitan is a vocational high school. Pupils are admitted on the basis of interest and, in the case of performing arts, evidence of talent in the selected field. Their academic ability is a secondary factor. The college preparatory work was originally placed in the school curriculum to meet the needs of continuation pupils who were also attending evening high school and who were looking forward to higher schooling. Subsequently, adults who were unable to go to evening school were permitted to enroll. With the introduction of the maritime courses, such college preparatory courses became a necessity for those pupils who planned to enter the United States Merchant Marine Academy or one of the state maritime colleges. The opportunity for college preparation was also sought by more capable pupils in the other vocational courses. In order to gain the recognition of the colleges, the school applied for and later obtained the regular secondary school charter from the State Board of Regents. Graduates who have taken the combined vocational and college preparatory courses have been readily admitted to colleges all over the country.

The school is truly metropolitan in other respects. Its pupils come from all five of the city's boroughs. A number travel long distances, by-passing high schools in their immediate neighborhoods, in order to enroll in the school's special courses.

The boys and girls are representative of all social and economic groups. Some come from homes on relief; others enjoy the security of a good family income. Side by side are students whose parents range from the illiterate, unskilled worker to the college-trained professional.

A visitor to the Metropolitan Vocational High School would have to tour through a considerable portion of lower Manhattan —and for the performing arts, visit the theater district in midtown—if he wished to observe all the school's activities. Besides its main building, which is situated in the heart of the new Alfred E. Smith Housing Development, Metropolitan has for classrooms one other school building, two public swimming pools, a public gymnasium, the Liberty Ship *John W. Brown* (moored at Pier 73, East River), and space in the headquarters building of the Western Union Telegraph Company.

Except for the swimming pools, the ship, and the gymnasium, these buildings were never intended for their present purposes. Two are old elementary schools, both of which underwent considerable alterations to adapt them to their new uses. The Western Union headquarters are excellent.

In New York City's long history as the nation's largest entertainment center, thousands of young people, from the superior to the most mediocre in terms of talent, have gone to private schools to receive instruction in the performing arts, usually after regular school hours in the late afternoon, evening, and on Saturdays. This instruction has varied in its quality from the best available to the most unsatisfactory. The Metropolitan Vocational High School, since instituting its work in the dance and drama (music had already been given on a vocational basis for some time), has come to render an invaluable service to talented boys and girls, who are thus able to combine their activities in these arts with their required schooling. Here, in the division known as the School of Performing Arts, the usual pattern of a half day in the vocational specialty and a half a day in academic work obtains. Four periods are devoted to each. The drive of these young people is clearly evidenced by the school's need to caution them and their parents against excessive application to their specialties after the school day is over.)

The enrollment in the Performing Arts Division is limited to 600, despite the fact that if all applicants were accepted it could readily be increased to several thousand.)One practical difficulty arises from the limitations imposed by the present building. However, this is merely physical and could be overcome. More important considerations are:

1. An appreciable proportion of applicants do not give immediate evidence of developing professional skill. While there would be considerable value in trying them out for a year or so, the results would not warrant the trial.

2. The performing arts are notably low employment areas, where only the highly talented and the lucky get jobs and even these are engaged only intermittently. The arts are obviously fields for only the naturally endowed and confirmed devotees. However, in a democratic school system such endowments and devotions must be served.

3. As it turns out, most, though not all, of these aspiring skilled performers have high enough intelligence (measured on the academic, verbal, or I.Q. scale) to succeed in college, and to college they go—(to colleges offering a generous allotment of time to music or drama or dance. The pupils are chosen solely on the basis of talent through auditions, first before members of the faculty (professional dancers, actors, and musicians) for the screening out of the obviously untalented, and then before members of the Advisory Commission (outstanding leaders in their respective fields) for the selection of top prospects among the survivors of the first screening.)Approximately one in four applicants is admitted.

Despite this selection purely on the basis of talent (for admission purposes the I.Q. and scholastic record are ignored), the median I.Q. of the September, 1949, entrants was 119.5, with a 50 percent range above that figure, up to 160.

This figure is particularly significant when compared with those in the Krugman-Wilson *Studies of Student Personnel.* Published by the New York State Education Department in January, 1951, this research paper, subtitled "The New York City Study of Vocational Education," surveys the I.Q. distribution of September, 1949, entrants to 81 New York City high schools. Inserting in that survey the School of Performing Arts figure compiled from the application forms of its entrants, the first nine city high schools in order of median I.Q. were:

1. Bronx H.S. of Science 141.5	5. Brooklyn Technical	118.7
2. Stuyvesant 128.0	6. Forest Hills	118.4
3. Music and Art 120.7	7. Samuel Tilden	114.3
4. School of Performing	8. Erasmus Hall	113.6
Arts 119.5	9. Midwood	113.5

The next highest vocational schools were the School of Industrial Arts, standing 42nd with an I.Q. of 99.2; Manhattan Aviation, 48th, with 96.0; Metropolitan (entire school), 51st, with 93.9; New York Printing, 55th, with 92.9; and Central Commercial, 57th, with 91.8.

The significance of these figures is that all five of the schools which lead the list select their pupils from the entire city on the basis of occupational talent (engineering, technical pursuits, music, art, dance, drama). While four are not officially designated as vocational schools, they actually belong in that classification. All prepare specifically for entrance to college.

The inference is clear: If all high schools provided for the education of the whole child (vocational, academic, social, cultural, etc.), and if advisors and counselors in elementary and junior high schools would guide their pupils to such schools in terms of the realities of human beings and of social demands, the correlation of vocational ability with verbal (academic) power would provide a new and revealing picture. Best of all, American youth would be getting a sound education.

Metropolitan's concern for the welfare of the individual pupil had its origin in the guidance program which it established in the East Side Continuation School. This program was in fact the *raison d'être* for the continuation school. It is fully as important in the full-time program, although the conditions under which it operates at present are not favorable to complete success.

Metropolitan has the services of a number of guidance specialists, two health counselors, a testing counselor, an attendance coordinator, and a head counselor, but the most valuable approach to the individual pupil is made by the pupil's homeroom teacher, his advisor. The pupil is assigned to an advisor at the time of his admission to the school, and this pupil-advisor relationship is maintained as long as both remain in school. The pupil meets the advisor each morning for forty minutes. On two of these mornings group guidance lessons, which are prepared by the head counselor, are taught. A third session is devoted to reports from the class delegate to the student's general organization.

In addition to these daily meetings, the advisor has one period a week specifically set aside for individual counseling in a room assigned for that purpose. The advisor is responsible for the pupil's cumulative record cards, and since they remain in his possession, their availability permits greater use than would ordinarily be the case.

The long and intimate contact between the pupil and his advisor makes it possible for the advisor to know each of his pupils as a personality. He is aware of particular needs. He makes the indicated referrals to the specialists in charge of various phases of school adjustment. He is, in truth, *in loco parentis*. Pupil after pupil has stated that his advisor was in many instances the one person who helped him over the hurdles not only in going through school but also in the solution of personal problems outside the school. The advisors in turn find that their guidance activities are the most rewarding features of their work as teachers.

Concern for the pupil as a total personality is further reflected in Metropolitan's curricular and extracurricular approach to high school education. The general educational values of English and social studies (which take approximately 50 percent of the time devoted to the academic and technical subjects) are enhanced by the pupil's vocational interests. The end results of cooperative enterprise, the existence of individual differences in productive skills, the role of the artisan in modern society, all become much more meaningful to young people in their studies in literature and history when they themselves are daily experiencing the discipline of occupational skills.

Metropolitan's progress makes provision for giving its pupils experiences in the amenities of social living. The pioneering efforts of Dr. Mary Sutton-Phelan in establishing and developing classes in personality training (for want of a better name) attracted considerable attention. Young people coming from cultural patterns and environments that handicapped them in their social relationships were given kindly, sympathetic, and highly skilled assistance in acquiring an ease in the niceties of everyday existence.

This class might be considered as another attribute of a school which regards vocational education as essentially education for life adjustment. The dynamics of vocational skills make it possible for the school to teach learning through living and to give the learner a day-by-day evaluation of his growth as an individual.

Some Comments. As with the programs of other schools represented in this and the following chapters, that of Metropolitan is offered for only one purpose—namely, to make clear the practical possibilities of organizing a vocational school (and that means *any* school) so as to satisfy both the occupational and cultural needs of students. The word "cultural" is here used in the sense that subjects required for college entrance are considered cultural, though this study has not tried to examine the cultural worth of the various college preparatory subjects. It may be that even for many highly intelligent children advanced mathematics and foreign languages are pure educational waste; but whether that be true or not, it certainly is true that, along with a vocation based on intense interest, the school can "give" these subjects and many of the students can "take" them.

A striking feature of the Metropolitan program is that, insofar as college preparation is concerned, it does in three hours—that is, half a day—what academic schools do in five or five and a half hours, and then goes on to give in another three hours—the other half of the day—a full shop program. This program conforms to the requirements of the Smith-Hughes Act as well as to the usual requirements set for admission by the colleges. So the college-gaited student has his cake and can eat it too.

In the usual sense of the word, Metropolitan is not a "comprehensive" high school. Despite many requests, it has consistently refused to offer a straight academic program without an accompanying shop program. Every pupil must prepare for a vocation and that vocation must be one of the restricted group offered by the school. However, *for those who meet these conditions,* Metropolitan offers a wide scope, a *truly* "comprehensive" program.

Mont Pleasant High School, Schenectady, New York

Mont Pleasant High School may best be described as a comprehensive high school. Within the same building are two major divisions: the Mont Pleasant Academic High School and the Mont Pleasant Technical High School, the latter separately approved as a technical school by the New York State Education Department. For the two divisions, the curriculum and program are so organized and administered that students of both the academic and the technical high schools are taught the academic subjects in the same classes. The technical high school pupils, who constitute about one third of all the boys, spend an additional part of the school day in the facilities assigned for the technical courses.

In Schenectady, as in any city, the secondary schools must

serve the needs of the whole community. This means that in addition to providing a core of general education for personal, social, and civic competence, the secondary school must cover a wide range of vocational objectives. These include college preparatory courses for liberal arts colleges; technical courses for engineering colleges or institutes; commercial courses for the business needs of the city; vocational courses for major and minor industries and trades, as well as diversified and general training for occupations where the more specific patterns of skills and abilities will be gained in a short period of on-the-job training.

The Mont Pleasant Technical High School is naturally influenced by two major industries situated in Schenectady—the General Electric Co. and the American Locomotive Co. The personnel needs of these two industries in vocational education are reflected both in the curricula of the day school and in the apprenticeship and extension program for post-high school training.

No curriculum or course of study in the Mont Pleasant High School is so rigid that changes cannot be made to fit the pupil for college or for commercial, technical, or other types of work; hence, a reasonable degree of flexibility is permitted the student who alters his educational or vocational purposes and goals.

The courses, or curricula, are set up to meet not only the needs of students but also the social, industrial, and economic needs of the community in which the school is located. Hence the school offers seven courses: college preparatory academic, technical electrical, technical mechanical, secretarial, cooperative retailing, clerical, and general high school.

The college preparatory course, intended for pupils who plan to enter colleges of arts and sciences, does not differ appreciably from those offered in other communities in New York State.

The technical electrical course and the technical mechanical course are both intended for pupils who are planning to enter into community industrial enterprises, such as the General Electric Co., the American Locomotive Co., the Niagara Mohawk Power Co., the New York Telephone Co., and the Mica Insulator Co. While the courses are designed so that boys may go directly into these industries from high school, a proportion of those students who have requisite ability and ambition proceed to engineering schools, colleges, or institutes of post-high school level. Of the electrical-course graduates 18.4 percent enter college, and of the mechanical-course graduates 14.6 percent. About 2 percent more work for a year or two and then go to college.

Admission into the technical courses is selective in the sense that individuals who wish to enroll in these courses must meet certain criteria of mental and physical abilities. No student may take the technical courses who has not done well in general science, algebra, and geometry. The student must also show a real and continuing interest in the particular course chosen. The courses of study within the technical school are conducted on a fairly high level. As a result, the students in the technical school maintain a favorable ratio of holding places of prominence among the comprehensive high school student body, on the school honor roll, as class officers, as chairmen of student committees, and in similar types of positions in cocurricular activities.

Pupils at the top of the classes in the commercial courses are accepted by some of the liberal arts colleges. Primarily, however, these courses prepare directly for work. The secretarial course, as its name implies, is designed to train students for jobs as stenographers and secretaries in business and industrial offices. The cooperative retailing course is intended for boys and girls who are interested in selling, particularly those who may later achieve positions in stores as buyers or department heads. Pupils in this course may work part time in a store in their twelfth year, and for satisfactory work experience, credit toward graduation is awarded. The clerical course is aimed at those students who wish to gain competence as typists and file clerks or in related office jobs.

The general course is designed to meet the needs of students who plan no further formal education. Pupils who, for a variety of reasons, cannot or do not wish to meet the requirements for enrollment in the college preparatory course, or the technical courses, are advised to register in this course, where a special interest or ability may be developed. These are the students most in need of a life-adjustment program. They are counseled to select subjects with great care so that each will be prepared for a more general type of work in some field when he is graduated. At present they may plan programs involving more elective subjects than are permitted students in other courses. These electives include art courses in drawing and painting; applied design work in clay, leather, metal, and enamel; advertising art and poster design. Music makes available training in choir, harmony, band, and orchestra. In the language arts are offered public speaking, dramatics, and radio and television workshops. In home economics there are classes in foods, clothing, and preparation for family life.

Besides its two big high schools, Mont Pleasant conducts a postgraduate apprentice division in the technical high school. Its normal enrollment of about 600 young men is divided among the following courses: (1) apprentice draftsman (in General Electric classes), (2) apprentice machinist (in General Electric classes), (3) technical course for laboratory assistants (in General Electric classes), (4) apprentice draftsman (for American Locomotive).

The enrollees, high school graduates, have generally been in the upper quarter of their classes in scholarship. Most are employed either by General Electric or American Locomotive, while a lesser number work for other smaller industries. All must attend school two hours a day, three days a week, forty weeks a year, and spend an equal amount of time on homework, for three years if they are draftsmen and machinists and for four if they are laboratory assistants. Many of these students are of college caliber, and a number are frequently allowed as much as a full year of advanced credit in some of the first-class engineering colleges.

For a city like Schenectady a high school thus organized and administered offers these advantages:

1. The students are allowed a maximum degree of flexibility in transferring from one course or curriculum to another course or curriculum better suited to their abilities and goals in education and vocational choice.

2. The fact that the academic and technical schools share the same building and participate in the same cocurricular activities permits the student body to have a balanced social program, since both boys and girls are living in the same comprehensive school.

3. Since both academic and technical school students take academic subjects such as social studies and English in the same classes, mutual understanding and regard for school achievement are engendered.

Because the technical classes frequently operate on a double-period basis, problems arise in integrating the schedules of the academic and technical students. However, they are always solved through appropriate administrative measures.

VOCATIONAL-TECHNICAL HIGH SCHOOL, BAYONNE, NEW JERSEY

Bayonne, New Jersey, is an industrial community of 93,000, about ten miles southeast of Times Square on upper New York Bay. Its population is made up largely of second- and third-generation Americans whose ancestors came from eastern Europe, Italy, and some of the western European countries.

The community has eighteen elementary schools—twelve of them public, and six parochial. Of the two public high schools, one is general, the other vocational-technical. There are also a parochial high school and a public junior college.

The vocational school was established in 1911, to furnish training to the youth of Bayonne who were "manually minded." With the passage of the Smith-Hughes Act it took on the usual pattern. In 1930 it was granted high school status by the State Board of Education, and its program in technical education was recognized by both the State Department of Education and the U.S. Office of Education.

The Bayonne High School has a business education course, a college preparatory course, and a general course. The Vocational-Technical High School is housed in an adjacent building and, in part, in the same building.

The High School and the Vocational-Technical High School have a common curriculum for the ninth year. Each offers English, history, general science, algebra or general mathematics, and mandated civics and health. In the Vocational-Technical School there are offered, in addition, a course in occupational information and one in preparatory shop—a different type of shop work each term and usually of the student's own choosing. The work in occupational information embraces, besides the usual lesson study of occupations, a visit to every shop and laboratory in the school as well as visits to local industrial plants. Some test work in mechanical aptitudes is carried on, and there are frequent opportunities for individual counseling. At the end of the ninth year, students may be transferred, without any penalty whatever, from the Vocational-Technical to the general high school, or vice versa, if it should appear that their educational needs would be better served by such a change.

For the purpose of state aid, this ninth year in the Vocational-Technical School is reported to the State Department of Education as a general education school. Reasons for the Vocational-Technical School's giving this work are first, it is felt that the students can receive better guidance and exploratory opportunities in the atmosphere of a vocational school; and second, it is believed that had they taken their ninth year in the general high school, they might have been influenced by loyalties to school, teachers, and classmates against making a transfer at the end of the year that would have been advantageous to their education and the realization of their career objectives.

The students who remain for the tenth year in the Vocational-Technical High School have thus been adequately screened and are definitely committed to the pursuit of education toward one of the many careers for which the school offers training. While the tenth-year curriculum differs somewhat for printing, dressmaking, beauty culture, and general industrial students, for all trade and technical courses it consists of English, materials of industry, intermediate algebra and geometry, applied physics, drafting, and shop work. The aim in the shop work is the definite determination of the trade to be studied; in it the student may begin to study his trade, or he may continue exploration if the determination has not yet been made.

Should any student care to transfer to the general high school at the end of the tenth year (as happens in rare instances), such transfer will be made with no penalties except those involved in meeting high school course requirements.

Specialization, i.e., actual trade training, is carried on in the eleventh and twelfth years. It has been found by experience that those students who are successful in ninth- and tenth-year mathematics and science will do well in technical work, and therefore the requirement has been set that a student shall have attained a mark of 80 percent or better in mathematics and science in order to pursue a technical course. As a matter of fact, not all who are in this group want to take technical courses.

An attempt has been made to duplicate fields of work in vocational and technical courses so that no student need feel frustrated in his career objectives if he cannot pursue a technical course. The technical courses are in power engineering, heating and ventilating, radio and electronics, industrial chemistry and laboratory assistant, metal trades and drafting, and electrical testing. The vocational courses are in automobile servicing, carpentry, patternmaking, electrical maintenance, dressmaking, beauty culture, welding, distributive fields, machine-shop practice, sheet-metal work, and printing.

By individual arrangements made with engineering colleges, graduates of the technical courses are accepted for admission to such colleges without having to meet the set requirements of each. Some graduates of trade courses who have made a change in career objectives as they neared graduation have been able to qualify for admission to general colleges. In fact, the curriculum of the ninth and tenth years of general education is so planned that the bulk of college entrance requirements can be met by either a trade or a technical graduate. Arrangements have also been made with the general high school in Bayonne so that students who wish to study a language, art, or any subject not offered in the Vocational-Technical school can be scheduled there.

The Vocational-Technical School is operated as a "three-level school." The technical courses represent one level; the skilled-trade courses, another level. Among students in the skilled-trade level there are two groups: those with I.Q.'s of 90 or over who are fully capable of absorbing the content of the courses in the skilled trades, and those with I.Q.'s of less than 80 who are unable to absorb the full content of the courses if they stay to graduate or who may leave school at the age of 16. Where it is definitely known that they will leave at 16, a general industrial course has been organized for handyman training, and there are also short unit courses in power-sewing-machine operation, manicuring, etc., so that the student will be able to complete a definite unit of instruction before he leaves. Where a student plans to stay to graduate, "A" and "B" courses have been organized in some of the trades so that each student can achieve to the measure of his ability.

The school has all types of athletic teams and competes in the State High School Interscholastic League in baseball, football, track, basketball, swimming, etc. There are also a school band, orchestra, dance orchestra, glee club, and instrumental-music instruction. Students put out a school paper and publish an annual, and their paper has often won first place in the Columbia Scholastic Awards. The pupils participate in all city and state essay, oratorical, and debating contests. Also available to students is an imposing list of clubs, among which are Radio, Camera, Debating, Dramatics, Chemistry, Journalism, Table Tennis, Dancing. There are frequent school dances, including the Senior Prom.

The school has a Placement Department, and an effort is made to see that every graduate and dropout finds work in the field of his choice and training. The same department attempts to supply jobs of a casual nature, after school hours, for those students who need financial assistance. A Supervisor of Apprentices assists graduates to make contacts for apprenticeship status and then for enrollment in organized trade extension courses in the evening in accordance with their particular needs. Graduates are followed up in their jobs, and the services of the placement department are available to any unemployed graduate at all times.

It should be emphasized that the school is intended only for those who wish to prepare for a career in some field for which the school is equipped to train. The curriculum is planned so that it will achieve several objectives:

1. To prepare the student with some saleable and marketable skill with which to earn a living.

2. To keep the "educational door" open so that the graduate who wishes to continue his education either in a day or evening school can be admitted to higher institutions.

3. To furnish a measure of education of a social and civic type, both through curricular and extracurricular activities, to prepare the student for social and civic as well as occupational competency.

4. To provide organized activities and experiences in the

school environment of a type that every American youth seeks, and to which he is entitled, while attending a secondary school.

CASS TECHNICAL HIGH SCHOOL, DETROIT, MICHIGAN

Cass Technical High School is a public school which prepares youth both for positions in industry and business and for admission to college or university. The school is fully accredited by the North Central Association of Colleges and Secondary Schools and affiliated accrediting agencies. In addition to its vocational and academic aim, Cass Technical High School is organized to achieve the common purposes of any high school—the cardinal objectives of education: to develop the young ideals and responsibilities of intelligent citizenship as well as individual ability and character. Many and varied student activities afford pupils an opportunity to practice civic behavior and to develop personal initiative and talent. Cass seeks to teach young people not only how to make a living, but how to live fully and well.

Through its Department of Health Education, Cass conducts for both boys and girls a complete program of health and physical education, including clinical service. Students may participate in all regular athletic activities, such as football, basketball, baseball, swimming, and track. R.O.T.C. may be substituted for physical education. And also available for student participation are school plays, dramatics, and instrumental and vocal music.

Because of the additional work required of Cass students, and because of the expensive and specialized shop and laboratory facilities and equipment, only those pupils can be enrolled whose qualifications indicate that they will profit most from the use of such equipment and facilities. The requirements, however, do not include any geographic boundary lines. Any pupil residing in Detroit is eligible if he (or she) meets these general eligibility requirements:

1. Satisfactory ratings in intelligence and vocational aptitude

tests. These tests are given to all pupils in Detroit public schools before they have completed the 9th grade. Others may arrange for such tests by appointment and without obligation.

2. Satisfactory completion of Grade 9A.

3. Recommendation of the counselor at the school last attended.

To graduate from Cass Technical High School, a student must have earned credits covering all requirements of the chosen curriculum. Pupils selecting a curriculum are supposed to consider the undertaking a contract to be met in all its specifications. The number of credits toward graduation, and the number of class periods per week, are prescribed for each subject in such curriculum contracts.

Students must have passing grades in all subjects to carry more than twenty hours per semester. Additional hours of credit may be carried if the counselor is satisfied with the pupil's ability to complete the work successfully.

Graduates of Cass may enter colleges of engineering, medicine, or dentistry; the liberal arts colleges; schools of applied science, nurses' preparatory schools, etc.—all according to the curriculum from which they have graduated. Since some colleges and universities require specific preparatory courses and exceptional scholarship for entrance, it is important that the high school student consult his counselor and curriculum head at Cass in regard to selection of courses. It should be noted that all curricula are "college preparatory" in nature. There are no "general courses" in Cass Technical High School within the day division of the school.

Graduates from any standard curriculum at Cass Technical High School may obtain employment as advanced apprentices in the field of their chosen vocations with the assurance that they have had a fundamental training upon which they can build successful careers. The standard curricula include aeronautics, air conditioning, architectural drafting and building, art, auto mechanics, home economics, mechanical and manufacturing, music, printing, and science.

In view of Detroit's position as center of the nation's automobile industry, Cass's automotive curriculum is most interesting.

The automotive mechanic or engineer deals with a complicated machine: one which involves practically every electrical, thermal, and mechanical principle. While it is possible to get a working knowledge of certain units of automotive maintenance and repairs through unit courses, the person who wishes to become an automobile mechanic should become thoroughly grounded in the fundamental principles of mechanics and science and have an intimate knowledge of the different units of the automobile. At Cass each year's work practically completes a unit in automobile construction. If it becomes necessary for a boy to drop out of school at the end of any year, he will at least have obtained training in the fundamentals of certain units of the automobile that should be useful in obtaining employment. Such courses as mathematics, chemistry, physics, and drawing are required of every student because these courses give a background for a thorough technical understanding of the automobile. Students graduating from this curriculum are eligible to enter universities or colleges of engineering.

With reference to the Cass program, the principal makes these additional points:

1. We have no Smith-Hughes classes in our day program. There are several reasons for this, but the sufficient one is that the time requirements of a three-clock-hour session in shop (15 hours per week) and a three-clock-hour session in "related work" is not flexible enough for our program. However, our adult classes are Smith-Hughes wherever possible.

2. Our day classes are completely acceptable to all colleges, and no special arrangements or dispensations are made. There is a salary

incentive for instructors with a Master's degree; all of the younger teachers are so qualified, as are most of the older faculty members.

3. For our class of January 1949, we reported that 53.3 percent of our graduates asked for college transcripts; for the class of June 1949, the percentage was 52.9. It should be pointed out that these percentages do not include transcripts for apprentice programs, and similar requests from other collegiate institutions. Obviously, too, they do not necessarily represent the fraction of graduates actually attending college.

4. I should like to emphasize the fact that we do not aim directly at college entrance. We plan that our graduates be employable at the technical level, and that such employability be achieved at an increasing level of competency as graduation is approached. The fact that Cass Technical High School is "unqualifiedly approved" by the North Central Association is because our graduation requirements happen to contain elements that coincide with the North Central requirements. We, of course, require more hours than are required from conventional schools, and often such courses carry extra credit in the new school attended. This again is a matter we do not point to, retaining our basic concern for "employability at the technical level and industrial welcome."

BOYS' TRADE AND TECHNICAL HIGH SCHOOL, MILWAUKEE, WISCONSIN

The Boys' Trade and Technical High School area is so organized as to satisfy both college entrance requirements and to give job training. In general, this combined academic and vocational course requires five years of work beyond the eighth grade. Greater emphasis is placed on technical and trade education. It does not operate under the Smith-Hughes and George-Barden Acts as do the vocational schools in Wisconsin, including the Milwaukee Vocational School. It should be noted, however, that the school is fully accredited with the North Central Association of Colleges and Secondary Schools.

Opportunities at the school follow in the wake of the following objectives:

1. To train for good citizenship.

2. To explore the abilities of the individual so that he may find his field of educational and vocational interest. This is done by offering exploratory vocational tryout courses, providing careful guidance, and by administering comprehensive tests, all of which shed light on the individual's abilities and interests.

3. To give craftsmanship training to those students who have shown interest and ability in a chosen vocation.

4. To provide appropriate training for those students who wish to attend a college or university.

5. To provide educational and vocational training for those students who wish to enter industry as technicians or advanced apprentices.

The Boys' Trade and Technical High School has these units: the Trade High School Division, the Technical High School Division, and the Trade-Tech Division. Within each is a wide enough range to permit any student possessing mechanical aptitude and interest to succeed in his chosen field.

The Technical High School Division differs from the Trade High School Division in that greater emphasis is placed on technical and academic training than on vocational training. Students graduating in this division may attend any accredited college or university, providing proper course selections have been made.

Only those students possessing interest and ability in purely academic areas are encouraged to select courses in the Technical Division. Both there and in the trade area, students have a rather wide selection. Students interested in technical work should naturally follow English and the sciences. Boys less inclined toward the foregoing may enter industry as apprentices. Others may find an allied field of vocational experiences through the media of work offered in this division. It is essential that good technicians possess a wide background of academic as well as vocational training.

Throughout the ninth grade in both the technical and trade areas, the work is exploratory in nature. In other words, boys are rotated every semester in four different areas of shop or drawing work. This is done so that the student may be reasonably sure that he has found himself vocationally and, beginning in the tenth grade, will have an opportunity to carry on in that field of work in which his interests and abilities lie.

A student may at the beginning of his tenth grade elect to enroll in (1) a trade course, (2) a technical high school course, (3) a combined trade and technical course, and graduate from any of the above divisions.

The Trade High School Division courses are particularly organized for students who wish to devote the greater part of their educational experience to the vocational areas, namely, shop and drawing.

Adjustments and electives may be incorporated in the trade work so that a boy may obtain a good portion of academic training as well as vocational training. This spread in organization is aimed to meet various levels of student ability. It should be noted that courses in this division are not college preparatory, but are primarily a preparation for vocational specialization after successfully completing the work in the trade area.

Some students who do not master the vocational skills in the average time period may be required to attend an additional semester, to cover completely the work experiences outlined in the respective courses.

The aim of Boys' Trade and Technical High School is to organize divisions for students of varied capacities, and it has been found through experience that a combination of the technical high school course and the trade high school course has proved advantageous both to students and to business and industry.

It was with that idea in mind that the school set up its Trade-Tech Division, in which boys who plan on finishing both courses may earn a combination Trade and Technical Division diploma. In general, this course requires five years of work beyond the eighth grade. Because of the extensive academic work involved in this third division, graduates of it ordinarily qualify for college admission, providing they complete the major and minor requirements. This course also permits boys who enter engineering schools to be admitted to advanced work in the shop and drawing areas.

In an era of average employment, it is difficult for youths under 18 years of age to find suitable employment. Hence, this division enables pupils who have not reached 18 to stay in school to take advanced work and finish their particular course. If the student wishes to follow this technical work in industry, a graduate of this division is always given credit as either an advanced learner or an advanced apprentice.

San Antonio Vocational and Technical High School, San Antonio, Texas

One of the three senior schools in the San Antonio school system, the Vocational and Technical School has as its purpose:

1. To prepare the student for a job, to help him secure that job, and to apply himself in it so that he can earn promotion.

2. To teach the student to think and to develop in him habits of study, the power of self-help, the capacity to learn, habits of work, and attitudes necessary for his future success.

3. To develop in the student sound health, worth-while avocational and recreational interests, intellectual curiosity, and joy in intellectual and artistic pursuits.

4. To awaken in the student a feeling of social consciousness and social responsibility, and to prepare him for successful participation in the civic and social life of his community, his state, and his nation.

The aim of the San Antonio Vocational and Technical School

is, therefore, to prepare the student to become a good citizen and a satisfactory worker and wage earner in industrial or commercial fields. This does not, however, exclude him from going to college should he desire to do so. Graduates of the school may go to college to continue their occupational training there.

Work in the school is divided into four main divisions: the Academic, the Commercial, the Part-Time Cooperative, and the Trade and Industrial. The Academic Division includes those subjects which are generally offered in any senior high school. The Commercial Division offers training in the basic fields of the business world. The Part-Time Cooperative Division offers an opportunity for students to attend school half a day. The Trade and Industrial Division includes curricula that afford training in trade and industrial occupations.

To enter the San Antonio Vocational and Technical School as a regular full-time student, a pupil must have completed the ninth grade of a twelve-grade system. Since the primary purpose of the school is to train students for employment in trade and commercial fields, only those academic students who live closer to the San Antonio Vocational and Technical School than to any other senior high school are accepted for enrollment.

The advisory room, sometimes called the homeroom, is the contact agency between the principal's office and the student body. It is the family group, so to speak, for the advisor is the sponsor and counselor of the students in a kind of parental relationship. A student is assigned to an advisor upon entering the school and remains with this same advisor throughout the time he is in school. Thus the advisor is acquainted with his personality, background, and individual problems. Since each student has the choice of two or three electives each semester, it is a particularly important duty of the advisor to help him work out early in his high school career his three-year program of study along the lines of his special interests and aptitudes.

The academic division or department is open to junior high school graduates who wish to pursue college preparatory work or to acquire the fundamental academic skills of expression, common knowledge, attitudes, ideals, and practices which are necessary for successful living in a democracy. It is also open to students who wish to do individual study in such special fields as vocal and instrumental music, music appreciation, journalism, homemaking, Spanish, pre-engineering, art and art appreciation, speech arts, and aviation science.

A student who plans to go to college must select his electives to meet the requirements for entrance into the particular college which he plans to attend. He should keep in mind that different departments within a college often have different entrance requirements. He must decide just what college and what departments he wishes to enter and plan his course of study to meet the requirements laid down by this institution of higher learning.

The vocational courses offered are pre-nursing, bookkeeping, business training, retail selling, secretarial, distributive education, architectural drafting, auto mechanics, cabinet, mill, commercial art, cosmetology, dressmaking, electrical trades, engineering, drafting, garment manufacturing, machine shop, piping trades, printing, radio, sheet metal, welding.

The Diversified Occupations program is a part-time cooperative training program in which school and industry cooperate in providing students with trade training. It was designed to maintain a close correlation between the subject matter being studied in school and the daily work experience of the student on the job, and to afford an easier transition from the school to the job. It was also planned to give students part-time cooperative training in any one of a wide variety of occupations, some of which are not offered in the all-day school. Training may be given for practically any occupation for which there is a definite need in the community and which requires at least 2,000 clock hours to learn.

Normally, a student enrolls in the Diversified Occupations program as a junior and signs a two-year training agreement. If, however, the student is a senior, and he has had two years of training in a day trade-shop course such as auto mechanics or machine shop, he may enroll in Diversified Occupations under a one-year agreement, provided that the field he enters as a part-time cooperative student is directly related to the field in which he trained as a day trade student.

PAUL HAYNE VOCATIONAL HIGH SCHOOL,
BIRMINGHAM, ALABAMA

The Paul Hayne School is one of Birmingham's six high schools, differing from the others in one important respect. Its chief purpose is to prepare young people, both boys and girls, for employment when they graduate. This definitely does not mean that there is no class work or book study, or that only vocational courses are given. The student also can take a curriculum leading to college entrance.

The following courses are given: auto mechanics, beauty culture, commercial art, drafting (architectural or mechanical), electricity, office practice, typing, shorthand, bookkeeping, calculating machines, machine shop work, printing (including linotype machine), radio, retail selling, tea room management, woodwork, cabinet making or pattern making, distributive trades, diversified occupations.

A four-year course, the curriculum provides for two years of the same subjects taught in the regular high schools of the city, followed by two years of specialized training for a selected occupation. During the first two years, while the student is earning his regular high school credits, he has the opportunity of trying out, in short periods, vocational courses in which he may be interested. He also studies the world of occupations, sees pictures of different kinds of work, and visits local industries. Thus he is helped to determine with more assurance the vocation for which he wishes to prepare in the second two years.

Beginning with the fifth semester and third year, the student spends one-half of each day (four 45 minute periods) working in shop or laboratory. For two other periods he studies the theory—the science, mathematics, and history—of his chosen vocation, and for two additional periods he studies the regular high-school subjects.

So, on finishing his four years of work at Paul Hayne, he obtains a high school diploma with sufficient credits to enter college without condition. Having had more than 1,000 hours of actual trade and business training, the student is likewise qualified to enter a number of technical college courses. He is also prepared for immediate employment. If a student does not wish to attend college, the school tries to place him in a desirable position for which he has been trained.

While many students do not expect to go to college, this combination of vocational training with high school studies holds open the opportunity of admission to college for those who later find they can attend. The general high school education obtained certainly broadens the vocational preparation and adds to the prospect of a successful career—whatever the occupation. And on the other hand, the practical work experience in a vocational shop will make a boy or girl a better engineer or artist or dietitian or accountant if the high school course is supplemented by college training.

Eighth-grade graduates who are interested in becoming skilled craftsmen or technicians and have the aptitude to profit from special training may make application to the principal for admission to Paul Hayne. Other qualifications are also considered. Since the school has the responsibility of recommending its graduates to industrial and commercial concerns which maintain high standards for their employees, it is concerned with the character, health, attitudes, and habits of its prospective entrants.

Students may also be admitted through the fourth semester by transfer from other high schools, if approved by the principal, without loss of credits. Regular high school credits earned above the fourth semester may not, in most cases, be substituted for vocational credits.

First-semester students usually come to Paul Hayne as a result of guidance in the elementary school. After two years of short tryouts in different occupational courses and classes to study the selection of an occupation, the student, toward the end of the fourth semester and after conferences with the shop instructor, determines finally the course he wishes to follow. Should he decide not to take a vocational course, he may transfer to the fifth semester at another high school without loss of credit. But if he wants to remain at Paul Hayne and his record is satisfactory, he enters the trade course of his choice.

The first semester in any vocational course is, in reality, a probationary period. If a student has clearly made an unwise choice at this point—despite all previous guidance—he is advised to change courses, even if it might cause loss of a few credits.

The final check on a student's ability and training comes during the eighth semester, when he is placed in a part-time job. If he succeeds at this job, the school feels no hesitation in issuing him a diploma.

Guidance is the very foundation of successful vocational training and is therefore given a major place in the school's program.

Students at Paul Hayne are given a health examination when they begin their vocational training. This measure contributes not only to their health and safety while in school but prevents possible rejection and disappointment when later they apply for full-time employment. One full period for each semester is also given to the study of safety, first aid, and general health problems.

The Paul Hayne School not only serves as a reservoir from which trained young people may be obtained for employment in a variety of nonprofessional occupations, but it endeavors—in cooperation with employers—to follow up and effect the best possible adjustment of the young worker to his job. A program of carefully supervised job placement, the school believes, is of paramount importance to the student in achieving ultimate job success. For the employer, the value lies in the elimination of loss sustained through poor adjustment or failure of the young employee in his work.

Experience in vocational training has shown that a period of three or four months of cooperative employment, during which a student spends part of his time at school and part at work, provides a most satisfactory opportunity for testing and adjusting. While working, the student is directly responsible to the employer like other beginners. Through the services of a vocational coordinator, the school is regularly advised of the student's work progress. If his performance is below par, he is returned to school for further training. If his work is satisfactory, he is allowed credit toward his graduation. All details of schedule, studies, etc., are arranged through conference between coordinator and company representative.

When a student has completed the four-year course at Paul Hayne School, he receives a regular high school diploma, with which he may enter college.

In some instances, upon approval of the principal, a student may be permitted to begin his vocational training in most courses after completing only two semesters of high school work. In such cases he receives a vocational certificate. Adults and high school graduates often attend classes for short and irregular intervals and are not concerned with graduation. Any adult, however, who meets the requirements for graduation may receive the diploma or certificate.

Trade organizations and employers in Birmingham have consistently endorsed the program of vocational training as offered through the Paul Hayne School by the Birmingham Board of Education. In consideration of this good will and support, the school has made every effort to restrict training to fields where it is needed. Many trade representatives have served on advisory committees and have aided in the preparation of instructional materials used in school shops. Trade committees and employers have also rendered service to the school in finding and recommending well-qualified men for instructors.

GERSTMEYER TECHNICAL HIGH SCHOOL, TERRE HAUTE, INDIANA

The Gerstmeyer Vocational School for boys was opened in 1915 under the auspices of the City Board of Education. Trade courses in woodwork, forge work, and drafting were offered in this, the original vocational school of Terre Haute. The Girls' Vocational School was opened in 1916 with trade courses in homemaking, millinery, and dressmaking. In 1922, the boys' school was moved to its present location, with an enrollment then of approximately 175 students. Thirteen years later, the girls' school also moved and joined the boys'—the two becoming a technical high school. The growth of the school since that time has been truly remarkable. A broad curriculum of studies is offered, and Gerstmeyer graduates are now taking their places efficiently in industry, in business, and in the professions. In enrollment, Gerstmeyer is now the largest school in the city.

Gerstmeyer serves the entire city of Terre Haute and is especially organized to meet the needs of two classes of students: (1) Any boy or girl regularly prepared to enter high school who desires to learn a trade and at the same time prepare himself or herself for a college course finds here the combined opportunity for these two types of work. (2) Any boy or girl graduate of the eighth grade may continue his or her schooling here, receive the benefit of vocational guidance through the combined resources of the school, and graduate with a regular high school diploma and with a maximum amount of trade training in a chosen occupation.

Students who complete the vocational course for boys meet the state requirements for high school graduation, and at the same time they are preparing for effective entrance into industrial employment. They are developing the marketable skills and gaining the related technical information which are required of industrial workers today. Boys who are planning to enter industrial employment after high school are encouraged to enroll in the vocational course. Most colleges will admit boys who graduate from this course.

Graduates of any of the courses (including vocational) are accepted in colleges, except where special requirements must be met; for instance, engineering courses in colleges call for more years of high school mathematics. About 25 percent of Gerstmeyer graduates go to college.

In addition to trade courses, Gerstmeyer offers the usual courses given in academic high schools. These include college preparatory, commercial, homemaking, general, music, art, and industrial arts. The following trade courses are offered: drafting, printing, machine shop, woodwork, foundry, auto mechanics, welding, electricity, and airplane mechanics, all meeting the Smith-Hughes requirements.

DERRY TOWNSHIP VOCATIONAL HIGH SCHOOL,
HERSHEY, PENNSYLVANIA

Derry offers the following courses: auto-body repair, carpentry, electricity, machine shop practice, plumbing and sheet metal, printing, and vocational agriculture. The program of studies is divided equally between academic and vocational courses in the tenth through the twelfth years.

Pennsylvania public secondary schools require for graduation the completion of a program of studies and activities which satisfies the minimum graduation standards of the Department of Public Instruction and the local school district.

In the vocational-industrial curriculum, Derry has certain requirements for graduation. Students enrolled in the vocational curriculum must carry on their roster the subjects listed in the program of studies plus any extracurricular activities in which they are interested. Graduation is based upon the achievement of three years of work in the tenth, eleventh, and twelfth grades, and a minimum of thirteen units is necessary. Of these thirteen units, nine must be satisfied by sequences which shall include one three-unit sequence and three of two units. Four ninth-grade credits are prerequisite to this requirement. Derry recommends that all students participate in as many of the musical, athletic, and extracurricular activities as possible, but of course they should not do so to the extent of neglecting regular school subjects. Club and extracurricular activities which are taken for credit are in addition to the thirteen units specified.

In order to be eligible for a high school diploma, the student must pass successfully all the subjects listed on the program of studies. A student who plans to enter college must contact the vocational director at the earliest possible time to ascertain the entrance requirements for the college curriculum to which the student desires entrance and to arrange for study in the evening school or the summer school to make up any deficiencies. Vocational students preparing for college entrance must complete the following requirements: plane geometry, American history, ninth-grade science, two years of senior high school science, ninth grade English, three years of senior high school algebra, advanced algebra, and two years of language—dependent on the college and course.

JOLIET TOWNSHIP HIGH SCHOOL AND JUNIOR COLLEGE, JOLIET, ILLINOIS

Joliet is a city with a population of somewhat more than 50,-000 located forty miles southwest of Chicago. It is largely an industrial city, but also serves as a trading center for a considerable area and supplies Chicago with a limited number of commuters. The Joliet Township High School and Junior College is organized on the township plan and includes in its district a substantial population living adjacent to the city. Elementary education is provided by a separate board of education for the city of Joliet and by boards in the other communities within the township.

The program of Joliet includes the high school, the junior college, the vocational-technical school, the summer school, and an adult evening school which includes naturalization classes. All these activities are administered by one superintendent and his assistants. Joint physical facilities are shared by all the programs. The summer school is used mainly for making up deficiencies incurred during the regular school year. The evening school offers for both high school and junior college students general and vocational classes that include work and trade and industrial courses.

The high school program covers six curriculum fields: general, college preparatory, commercial, homemaking, trade-industrial, and vocational agriculture. Within these fields there is opportunity for considerable specialization. The trade-industrial student may elect auto mechanics, drafting, electric work, machine-shop practice, printing, or woodworking as his major field.

All curricula, including the vocational, require ten units in general education. All students take three years of English, besides social studies, world history, United States history, general mathematics, biology, and earth science. All boys must take general shop (industrial arts)—which provides a rotation through the several vocational shops—and all girls must take home economics. Both sexes are required to have health and physical education each year plus a health-problem course which runs one semester and may be taken in either the eleventh or twelfth year.

Certain aspects help unify the school and avoid segregation of pupils within curriculum areas. All students take the same program in the ninth grade; the differentiation begins the following year. The length of the school day—from 8:25 A.M. to 3:45 P.M.—is the same for all students, whether academic or vocational. The numerous extracurricular activities are also open to all students. In the general education courses, vocational students mix with those pursuing academic curricula.

The range of course offerings is great. Besides the general shop courses, which all boys must take in the freshman year, the school offers further work in industrial arts in the woodworking and drafting fields during the sophomore year. Special elective courses include journalism, dramatics, fundamentals of radio, corrective speech, photography, aeronautics, remedial reading, problems of our democracy, and world geography.

The vocational-industrial program is patterned on the Smith-Hughes formula, with three hours of shop work a day, related science, mathematics, drawing, art, and general education courses. Vocational programs in auto mechanics, electrical work, machine-shop practice, and printing start with the tenth year and continue for three years. The woodworking and drafting programs start with the eleventh year and are two years long. In the tenth year, the general education courses are English and general mathematics, and the related work is industrial drawing for all except printing majors, who take industrial art. In the eleventh year, the general education includes biology and world history; the related work is shop mathematics. In the twelfth year, the student takes English and United States history, plus related work in physical science. No attempt is made to segregate related content by specific trades, but the related-work applications are worked out for the various trades represented.

All shops are well equipped; new equipment has recently been installed in the machine shop, and facilities for industrial electronics and television added to the electrical program. In the spring term of 1950 the shop courses attracted more than 50 percent of the boy sophomores.

The junior college offers lower-division or transfer programs for those pupils who desire to go on to the University of Illinois or other higher institutions. It also offers terminal curricula for those who expect to enter employment on completion of junior college. Recently, the vocational shops have been opened to such students, and the enrollment of junior college students in vocational-industrial programs is increasing. The vocational programs include the commercial and distributive fields as well as the industrial.

Considerable emphasis is placed on music and on various extracurricular activities in the institution as a whole. Vocational as well as other students may carry a unit of band, orchestra, choir, or chorus in addition to other courses, and these musical activities may also be taken as elective majors. Seven different musical organizations are included in extracurricular activities. Interscholastic and intramural athletics play an important part. Altogether there are 21 clubs of various kinds open to high-school students.

The Joliet Township High School and Junior College seems

to have found a way to serve the greatly varied student body in meeting vocational needs as well as those of general education in a unified comprehensive program on both the high school and junior college level.

HADLEY TECHNICAL HIGH SCHOOL, ST. LOUIS, MISSOURI

The primary function of this school is to provide educational experiences for students who want training so they can get jobs immediately on graduation. College entrance requirements may also be fulfilled if the student decides a year or more before his graduation. Approximately 1 percent of the graduates indicate an interest in, or apply for, admission to college. Several colleges and universities will accept graduates with deficiencies in mathematics and some other subjects.

The following courses are offered: aeronautics, auto mechanics, commercial art, commercial cooking, cosmetology, drafting, electricity, machine shop, millinery, printing, radio, sewing and tailoring, welding, woodworking, bookkeeping, general clerical, stenography.

All courses except bookkeeping, general clerical, and stenography meet Smith-Hughes requirements and are approved by the State Department of Vocational Education.

Students are admitted upon graduation from the eighth grade. The general requirement for graduation from the Hadley School is a minimum of 36 term credits (18 units) of which 4 term credits (2 units) may be free vocational or academic electives.

Every effort is made to keep the training geared to the requirements of business and industry. This is accomplished through advisory committees from business and industry, the employment of instructors with five or more years of trade or business experience, and the requirement that these teachers maintain sufficient contact with their fields of work on the outside to enable them to keep abreast of all the changes.

WILLIAMSPORT SENIOR HIGH SCHOOL,
WILLIAMSPORT, PENNSYLVANIA[1]

A High School Technical-Vocational Curriculum.   A per-
plexing problem in secondary-school administration is involved
when the usual Smith-Hughes vocational course cannot be made
to meet the full needs of the pupil who wishes to follow a vocational curriculum and also prepare himself for college. In the
Williamsport, Pennsylvania, Senior High School, where Dr. L. F.
Derr is the principal and Dr. Paul E. Whitmeyer is the Superintendent of Schools, this problem has been met for some twelve
years by a simple administrative device.

At the senior high-school level, most pupils should have terminal occupational training, since six out of seven will not participate in any formal education beyond high-school graduation.
At the same time, it does not seem in keeping with our American way of life to bar any youth from college work because he has,
in his earlier years, followed a vocational curriculum. Also, in
spite of many speeches to the contrary, the Smith-Hughes mandated occupational training objective is to be met. The solution
lies in keeping the vocational program, with its high skill standards, intact and adding the extra academic training for those
who have the mental ability, drive, and probable financial resources to follow a technical college program later in life.

After an observation period of one year, or at the close of the
tenth grade of the three-year vocational course, selected pupils
are nominated by the faculty as apt candidates for the technical
course, which operates within the frame-work of the vocational-
industrial course. Selection takes into consideration test scores,
school marks, previous education, and other indications of pos-

[1] An excerpt from an article by George H. Parks, Director of the
Williamsport Technical Institute, is here presented. The article was
published in the *Bulletin of the National Association of Secondary-School
Principals*, May, 1950.

sible leadership qualities. The most important criterion is the opinion of the faculty as to potential ability and working spirit. The course is well known in pupil circles as a rigorous one, and sometimes the faculty has to "sell" the course to a given candidate. For the most part, the pupils accept the nomination as an honor.

The course is a "bargain" in that the full objectives of a strong vocational course are available, and, at the same time, a reasonably strong college preparatory program may be accomplished. The college preparation is limited to those colleges of engineering or technology which do not require a language for admission. The combined vocational and college preparatory course may be completed within the three-year high-school period—thus the educational bargain.

A Privileged Group. The technical course pupils are privileged to work far harder than those following the straight vocational curriculum. The type of pupil who enters this course is capable of much more sustained effort than the usual secondary-school program imposes upon him. He will literally jump any hurdle you place before him, and, as has been said often enough, that hurdle is not high enough for the superior pupil. The technical pupils are expected to do much better in their usual classes, to accept a more difficult assignment, and to achieve more in every respect. Their school day is longer than that of other pupils, usually to the extent of two hours of evening attendance a week. They may also be asked to attend a special program in the summer, although this is not usual. Boy-like, of course, the technical pupil complains about his hard life, his long hours, and his difficult subjects, but he loves it. He is a marked man. He belongs to the high school equivalent of the robed society of distinguished scholars.

The Curriculum. The standard vocational curriculum consists of fifteen hours per week of shop work, six hours of English and general mathematics as related subjects. [See Appendix 6.]

To these are added for college preparatory purposes, four additional hours per week each semester of general studies, two hours per week of mathematics, and two hours per week of science. Considerable attention is given to mathematics and science as being most indicative of future success in engineering studies. The eleventh grade pupils take chemistry and social studies the first semester in evening school and mathematics and English are given the first semester while physics and social studies are offered the second semester. By this arrangement, boys receive a minimum of 125 clock hours of instruction in mathematics, social studies, and English and 160 clock hours in science, including laboratory work. Classroom work in science is done during the day; and laboratory work, in evening school.

The Results. The results have been excellent. A total of approximately 368 pupils have been graduated from the course in the past twelve years since it was begun. No complete records of the graduates are available, but each year a substantial number enter college.

The Terminal Results. As expected, most of the graduates of this vocational-technical course do not go on to college. For them the combination of vocational and college preparatory training opens the door to the better jobs in private employment. These graduates are slowly emerging as the key leaders in the working life of the community. Usually they return to the advanced technical course offered by the school district in its Technical Institute and thus move upward on the managerial ladder. As a matter of record, many of these terminal graduates do even better in the industries of the community than their fellows who continue through college. Those who do not enter college have become evening-school conscious through this program. They tend to keep coming back year after year "to build themselves up," both vocationally and avocationally.

VII. Who Are These Boys and Girls?

A chapter of miniature profiles

Education is boys and girls. It is not a list of subjects or a manual of methods or specifications for buildings. It is not English, history, woodworking, or even teachers. It is small fry and gangling youth—your kids and my kids—troublesome, adorable, pains in the neck, and precious jewels—all trying to grow up and already bossing us around. They are, above all, individuals. The only safe generalization is that each one is different.

So, in a book about large schools, thousands of pupils, courses, subjects, classes, all implying some likenesses among children, we can really get down to the fundamentals of education when we talk about your son and my daughter and the little boy who lives down the street. This is a chapter about individual, very particular, boys and girls.

We have emphasized the fact that this is a book about free youth. *Free* youth, of course, are youth who are free to learn, free to do, free to speak, whatever they *can* learn, do, and speak. They must be free to learn any honorable occupation, and must be free to follow that occupation after they have learned it. They must be free to change their minds about occupations and free from outside pressures to divert them. They must be free to fulfill their great desires. They must be free to serve other people.

One day Margaret Webster talked most truly and excitingly to the boys and girls in the School of Performing Arts. She drew her text from Agnes de Mille's book, *Dance to the Piper*. After a life of many disappointments Agnes had just made her big hit in choreographing *Oklahoma*. While she was talking to the young man to whom she was to be married, the telephone kept ringing and ringing, "MGM wants you. . . . Paramount is interested. . . . Sam Goldwyn is really interested."

"I spoke to my mother. First I told her I was going to get married soon, and then I told her about the Hollywood money. 'I can pay you back everything. I can help now. I can be a real help.'

" 'What are the terms?' she asked.

" 'A seven year contract . . .'

" 'Never,' she shouted through the phone. 'Never, not for any money. Your freedom is not to be bought for anything in the world. Not for money. Keep your freedom. It is beyond price. You must be able to choose. Do not consider the money. Think only of the kind of work you want to do. Don't ever speak to me about paying back.'

"Oh, Annie! Spoken like your father's girl! She had done without every possible luxury to keep me going, a woman aging and sickening fast. I listened to her as I had grown used to doing. When she spoke, the bugles called."

For the most part, this book describes educational environments that purport to give just this kind of freedom to young people. However, what the boy and girl want to know, what their parents want to know, what teachers, principals, superintendents, and Boards of Education should want to know, is, what actually happens to the pupils in these schools? Do they really have freedom? Do they make good choices? Do they get good jobs? Do they work honorably, effectively, in the interest of both themselves and their fellow men? In other words, are these schools providing effectively for individuals in a democracy of many other individuals? The rest of this chapter will tell about real boys and girls (now men and women) who have attended the twelve schools which we have been describing.

First, a word about the form of presentation. We have called these stories "miniature profiles." They could also be histories, characterizations, close-ups, or thumb-nail sketches. We like the word "profile," even when reduced to miniature, because the professionally written profile of *The New Yorker* is based almost solely on the subject's occupation. And so are our profiles. True, our young people have not yet established great reputations. They have not lived long enough to become authorities, but as far as they have gone, they have lived intensely, have been motivated strongly, and are looking forward eagerly to important places in the life of the world. They are some parents' sons and daughters. If they were our own children, their stories would be fascinating history. As a matter of fact, to their principals their stories *are* fascinating histories. And if they were *your* children, they would be the most precious of documents.

Lincoln Barnett, in his fascinating book[1] suggests an interesting motivation for the closeup. "The deep underlying reason for the popularity of the personal sketch is the biological fact that man vastly prefers the contemplation of himself to any other object. . . . It was the motivation of Plutarch, who invented the technique of the closeup towards the end of the first century A.D. Contrary to popular belief, Plutarch was less concerned with 'lives' than with character and employed biographical details selectively to that end. 'It was for the sake of others that I first commenced writing biographies,' Plutarch observed in a self-revelatory moment, 'but I find myself proceeding and attaching myself to it for my own; the virtues of these great men serving me as a sort of looking-glass, in which I may see how to adjust and adorn my own life. . . . We receive, as it were, in our inquiry and entertain each successive

[1] Lincoln Barnett, *Writing on Life: 16 Closeups*, New York, William Sloane Associates, 1951.

guest and select from their actions all that is noblest and worthiest to know. . . . Ah, and what greater pleasure can one have?' "

So, in a "sort of looking-glass," as parents, teachers, citizens, we see how we may adjust and adorn our own lives in the interest of these boys and girls. Let us see what we see.

THEY CHANGED THEIR MINDS

The outstanding characteristic of the double-purpose school is the readiness with which it adapts itself to the needs of highly differing pupils and enables them to reach diverse goals. Moreover, it is favorable to the highly sensitive individual who, as he extends or integrates his education, understands himself better and changes his mind as to goal; all roads are kept open to his striving. Our first boy imagined himself as an electrical engineer but turned out a doctor. Our second boy pictured himself as a commercial photographer but became a Presbyterian minister. Our girl aimed for the stage but is now specializing in the teaching of the deaf. All three realized their desires through a double-purpose school.

The head of the Mont Pleasant Technical High School in Schenectady tells about the doctor:

We have a great number of boys who have graduated and gone on to college and, too, in the course of events have done outstanding jobs in many different lines of work. The usual thing is for a boy to take an electrical course in technical high school, to go on to engineering college and come out as an electrical engineer. However, this boy took the electrical course in high school and then went on to college and came out a doctor. Alfred M. Stineman became interested in the school through a friend and later his parents moved to Schenectady and remained here while he attended high school and was graduated with honors in January, 1941. This, of course, was at a time when he was most certain to be taken into the Armed Forces, so Al decided it would be more sensible to enlist and choose his branch of service. After due consideration he decided to join the Navy. He was assigned to the hospital section of a battleship.

Up to this point Al had had no thought whatever of becoming a doctor, but the medical men discovered that he was quite expert in the handling of various electrical devices and instruments, such as electro-cardiographs. It was through this association with the doctors that he finally concluded he would like to become a doctor himself. After the war, when he was honorably discharged by the Navy, he decided to use the aid due him under the G.I. Bill for the purpose of attending college. He therefore entered the University of Oklahoma and completed his pre-medical training. On graduation from Oklahoma he entered Long Island Medical College. During his work at the medical college Al decided that he was not particularly interested or gifted in surgery, but that he would be happier and much more successful if he became a heart specialist. This he did.

About two years ago Al dropped into the office just to say "Hello." He had always been anxious to revisit the school and some of his friends in Schenectady, and also to say goodbye as he was on his way to Korea to serve in the medical corps of the Armed Forces as a doctor. At that time I suggested that since he had become a physician, perhaps he would have done better to have taken an academic course while in high school, whereupon he gave me a very decisive "No," adding that, had he taken an academic course in high school, he never would have become a doctor, because it was entirely through his knowledge of electrical instruments and radio devices that he became interested in medicine. He is now specializing in a branch of medicine in which the successful use of intricate electrical instruments plays a very important part. For example, when he now takes a cardiogram of a heart patient he can immediately tell whether it is the cardiograph or the heart that is out of kilter. He has seen some cardiograms diagnosed as a peculiar heart ailment where the heart apparently was not too bad, but the instrument was decidedly defective and the one demonstrating it did not know the difference.

It was a great pleasure to note the real development in Al's general bearing and manner, and the splendid effects of the combination of maturity and mental training. He still has the fine personality that will be a wonderful assistance to him as a doctor.

Charles Gensheimer spent four years in Metropolitan Vocational High School preparing to be a photographer, with excellent prospects of being an exceedingly good one. His teacher reported that "a class of boys like Charles would be a joy." He was "conscientious, reliable, trustworthy, cooperative." Almost to the very end he wavered as to the type of photography in which he would specialize, but with a definite leaning toward radiology. But then some spiritual force moved him. It seemed to express itself in a poem he wrote for the school paper, "Democracy's Soldier—Upon Hearing of the Death of Franklin Delano Roosevelt." The last stanza:

> His spirit lives in us still,
> And when the battle is won
> He'll reach to touch each heart,
> He'll whisper, "My land, well done."

Charles's heart reached out. And this is how he tells it:

Although I studied Commercial Photography at Metropolitan, I did not continue my studies in that field. However, I am not intimating that my years in the Commercial Photography department were wasted. On the contrary, I know that they were good years in my life.

After graduating from Metropolitan in January of '46, I began my undergraduate work at Westminster College in New Wilmington, Pa. I graduated with a B.A. degree in June of '49. Feeling called to the Gospel Ministry, I entered Pittsburgh-Xenia Theological Seminary in Pittsburgh, Pa., from which I graduated with a B.D. degree in May of '52. At present I am serving as an Assistant Pastor in the Cherry Hill United Presbyterian Church here in Dearborn.

In my experiences at Metropolitan, I realize now that I received a broad academic-vocational education, and because of the very nature of Metropolitan, a real social understanding as well. I am especially grateful for my advisor, who did a great deal in steering me in the right direction. I was happy to see when I visited recently that the old neighborhood had been torn down. It was wonderful to see the new and bright community around our school.

Ellen Weiler was born in Berlin where she and her parents suffered all the indignities of the Nazi regime. However they managed to get to the United States when Ellen was five, before the great blow fell. In due time she passed her audition for admission to the School of Performing Arts. "I was terribly excited and that excitement has never entirely subsided." Acting was always in her mind. In the school production of *Green Grow the Lilacs*, the play upon which *Oklahoma* was based, she played Aunt Eller. The chairman of the Drama Department then wrote:

DEAR ELLEN,

I want you to know, at graduation, what a pleasure it has been for us to have you as a student in the Drama Department. We all have the highest regard for your outstanding personal qualities of quiet charm, maturity, intelligence, understanding, integrity, ability, application, cooperation and professional attitude.

Ohio State University is fortunate to be getting you. We shall be most interested in following your career, watching the full development of your abilities and of the acting talent we know you to possess.

However, Ellen too had a vision. The glamor of the stage receded while a career as teacher of the deaf took its place. No finer personality could offer itself to the handicapped. No better basic equipment could be provided than in the dramatic arts. Nor could Ohio State University be honored by a worthier student.

THEY KEEP THEIR EYES ON THE BALL

The most common course of events is for a boy to be attracted to a double-purpose school by the opportunity to work in a shop, to plunge into the handling of electrical material, of machine tools, of wood and metal and cloth and plastics—to become a craftsman. Then, according to his tastes and understanding, he progresses to theory and general principles and mathematics and science. Before he knows it, he is on his way to becoming an engineer. He goes on to a technical college and to his profession with this advantage over his colleagues who have been wholly technically trained—he knows how to use his hands. Instances of such experiences fill the records of these schools.

In the Mont Pleasant Technical High School Robert W. Mayer was such a boy.

He took our electrical course, was popular enough to be elected president of the graduating class for the whole school (academic and technical divisions), which at that time numbered about 2,000 boys and girls. The Technical Division had only a third of those boys, so our group could never elect a president entirely on its own. For a technical boy to be elected he had to possess definite qualities of leadership and to be the type of personality attractive to academic people as well as technical people. Bob was the first one we sent to M.I.T. on a full tuition scholarship. He was a top-grade man all the way through the cooperative electrical engineering course, which he finished with high honors and a Master's Degree. Bob has done an outstanding job as an engineer down at the Works and has contributed a great deal to the design of special controls and other apparatus which were invaluable in connection with the winning of the war. In fact, two years ago he with two other men were cited at a ceremony in New York City by the Electrical Engineering Fraternity as the three outstanding engineers for the year 1950 in this country and Canada. He was also cited a year or two before that by the General Electric Company for outstanding service and was given what is known as the Coffin Award for this service.

Last year Bob and a co-author named Harold Chestnut published a book on servo-mechanisms which is one of the very first of its type on the market. He is now working on a second volume of this book which has to some extent revolutionized this branch of engineering. Yet, with all this, Bob is a very modest chap and finds time to meet with our Tuesday noon luncheon group from the MPTHS Alumni Association. We have also called upon him many times to serve in the capacity of counselor for boys coming in from junior high schools. He contacts the parents as well as the boys and has given excellent counsel. Two years ago he spoke at the Milwaukee A.V.A. meeting of the American Technical High School Association.

The story of Anthony D. Mustillo at Bayonne (N.J.) Technical High School is much the same. Now a senior at the Newark College of Engineering, he gives great credit to his high school for its philosophy of technical education. Harold Engelhardt, another Bayonne student, is working at Purdue University for a degree in civil engineering.

Metropolitan trains boys for the sea. The larger number ship out immediately after graduation in the lower unlicensed jobs of ordinary seaman, wiper, or messboy. (All radio boys must and do obtain licenses and sail as full-fledged operators.) The more capable and persistent of these boys work their way up "through the hawsepipe" and become licensed officers. The best of them reach the top as masters. However, there is a faster and more satisfying route for those with a love of science and mathematics and liberal arts. They enter one of the half-dozen maritime colleges in the country and graduate after four years with a third mate's ticket and the rank of ensign in the Naval Reserve. The double-purpose high school prepares them for entrance.

Dennis Daley graduated from the United States Maritime College and is a captain for the Farrell Lines. Alvin Brand graduated from the same institution and is a lieutenant in the Navy. Alexander Kaufman graduated from the N. Y. State Maritime College. William Gunn has just graduated from Maine Maritime College and Bertram Magnus will soon follow. An interesting comment on all these boys is their outstanding records in every phase of character. They are the stuff out of which great shipmasters are made, men to whom passengers can entrust their very lives. Lennart G. Holmberg sums up neatly what most of these maritime boys would say about the double-purpose school.

My basic reason for coming to Metropolitan was due to the fact that you offered a course in radio, and at the same time I would be able to get a college preparatory course. The shop work was definitely the greatest attraction to the school as far as I was concerned. I probably would have attended an academic high school, although at the time I entered high school that was my greatest problem. I could not decide between a trade or a college prep course. I definitely wanted both.

I majored in Physics and minored in Chemistry and Mathematics, both Physics and Chemistry required many hours of laboratory work and I definitely enjoyed these courses most. While attending school I did a considerable amount of radio repair work for friends and neighbors. This work helped in financing my way through college although I was being sent through by the Government under the Veterans School Program. After I graduated with a B.S. I re-entered the U.S. Navy where I had been and now am working in the field of communication and radar. I am at the present time an Aviation Electronics Officer.

Unquestionably in my own personal experience, the study of electricity (electric wiring and motors) and the radio repair shop plus the course in typing have been most useful to me. This of course does not mean that many of the other useful things I learned and/or developed at Metropolitan have not come in for their share of use, but I do believe that much of the academic studies were more for preparation in future studies and after using them as stepping stones could be discarded, while on the other hand, skills developed in the shops were more practical and need not be discarded. I cannot think of any that I could have done without, but rather, I wish I could have taken even more. I consider myself quite successful as far as I have gone at the present time. I have chosen the U.S. Navy as a profession and therefore have available to myself all the educational facilities of the Navy. I have been to a number of these schools already and am at the present time attending a thirty-weeks course in various electronics equipment used by the Navy Air Force.

I have had many opportunities to be thankful that I attended Metropolitan. Ever since I can remember I have had two interests, radio and the sea; Metropolitan was the beginning of training for both. When I joined the Navy I had no trouble in getting assigned to radio work and as I advanced in rate and responsibility I began to enjoy it even more, but when the war was over I decided I had better go to college. After college I again entered the Navy and it was at that time I decided to make it a career. I had found what I consider for myself the fulfillment of my earliest ambitions, the sea and radio.

My opinion on the double-purpose school is this: I am all for it. I have had personal contact with several men, who, for one reason or other, had to disenroll from college. Had these men had some type of trade training, they could easily have gotten good jobs in these fields with the additional education they had acquired, but because of the lack of training in *anything*, these men had to start at the very bottom of a trade or profession, probably professions they did not prefer. My personal knowledge of a few men could probably be multiplied by every college in the country to give you an idea of how many persons would have benefited greatly by a trade training. At the same time, I am not to be misunderstood as stating that everyone should have a trade. There are many occupations that definitely do not require the type of training offered by the double-purpose schools, but generally, the average student in our society today would do well to obtain this type of training. It certainly pays off in the future, I can personally vouch for that.

The principal of the Milwaukee Boys' Technical High School reports on two boys who have followed this high-school-to-college arrangement:

A carefully arranged curriculum and a wisely adjusted guidance program have made the Boys' Technical High School, Milwaukee, perhaps the outstanding "double-purpose" technical high school of the middle west. Here a young man may prepare himself to earn a living directly upon graduation. At the same time he is afforded a valid preparation for continuing advanced training in college.

Typical of Boys' Tech's graduates is student Wilhelm Steffe, who early in his school life showed an interest in and aptitude for work in the electronics field. Wilhelm wasn't sure he could go on to college, so he chose Boys' Technical High School for his training for direct entry into industry. Upon entering Boys' Technical High School, his technical work in electronics encouraged him to study also in the fields of mathematics and sciences to enrich his vocational training. He planned his program so that he could either go on to college or take an advanced training course in industry as a technician. He entered Boys' Tech in 1949, graduating as salutatorian from the electrical course in June, 1952. Fortunately, he obtained a scholarship at the University of Wisconsin and is now enrolled in electrical engineering there. He has found the technical information he acquired at Boys' Tech of material help in his college pre-engineering work. He also has an excellent academic background, but feels the technical knowledge he received in high school is of even greater help in pursuing his college studies. While in high school, he was also able to gain considerable experience by working part time in his chosen field at a local radio supply company. He chose his high school wisely and was prepared for industry or college.

Jack Lemanczyk, a graduate of 1948 from the aeronautics department, is another example of the value of a broad technical curriculum in preparation for college or a position in industry. Jack had a rather poor financial background and home environment, but after graduating with honors from Boys' Tech, he obtained an excellent scholarship and continued his studies in electrical engineering at the University of Wisconsin. He is to graduate next June from the university where he has maintained high scholastic standing. This has enabled him to maintain his scholarship throughout his college career. He felt that his excellent mathematics training at Boys' Tech was of inestimable value in his college engineering work, and as a result he has maintained a straight A average in college math. He also found time for extra-curricular activities in athletics and is a lieutenant in the ROTC.

They Work Their Way Through College

For the academically inclined boy, working one's way through college is an old story. Waiting on table, stoking furnaces, cutting grass, coaching other students—all these add up sometimes to board and tuition. However, training for a remunerative job and at the same time preparing for college is a newer story—a most plausible and satisfying one. Michael Petrilak tells, in a long, exciting account, how he did it. We print his letter in somewhat abbreviated form:

In junior high school I had read many books about the sea, and decided to attend M.V.H.S. so that I could learn radio operating and sail in our Merchant Marine. I had developed an interest in electricity earlier and wanted to follow along that line. I had thought I would go to an academic high school and then join the Navy, but my eyes were too poor to be accepted so Metro was exactly the school to attend to fulfill my dreams of the future. It wasn't the shop work that particularly attracted me, but the curriculum in general that interested me; an academic and vocational training—especially when the vocational training was of a maritime nature! I would not have gone to a purely academic high school. In fact, I now recall, that I had thought of going to Haaren Vocational High School until I learned of Metropolitan Vocational High School's maritime training. You gave quite sufficient college preparation; however I noticed that 90 out of 100 students taking the academic courses did not take the regents, because they did not entertain the slightest idea about going to college; those who did and took the regents in general did poorly.

You know that I graduated as Valedictorian—I always did well in shop (all "excellents") because I like (always) to work with my hands as well as with my head. I had obtained my 2nd Class Commercial Telegraph and First Class Telephone F.C.C. Licenses by 6th term, and spent the Senior Year shop time helping my teacher. At any rate it was after I had obtained these licenses that I decided to attend college, for my interest in electronics had been greatly increased by your training. I graduated in June 1946, and had attended part-time during that last semester and from September to January 1947 Seward Park High School so that I could take certain courses that we did not (rightly so!) offer (e.g., Advanced Algebra, Solid Geometry, Earth Science). I took the Entrance Examinations to both City College of Engineering (competitive status) and Brooklyn College. I was accepted by both, but decided to attend Brooklyn as it was closer and after completing their 2-year pre-engineering course to transfer to CCNY for their Engineering (electrical) curriculum. However, I liked Brooklyn so much and had become interested in the Pure Sciences more than in applications, so I majored in Physics and minored in Math.

You can see that the period from January 1947 to June 1952 is 5½ years; I graduated this June (1952) with a B.S. in Physics; the reason for that is that I had to "work my way through college." I actually spent 7 semesters in B.C. plus 2 summer sessions; the remainder of the time was spent earning and saving money to support myself and send myself through college. My folks were unable to help, financially that is. To make the point—I earned my keep the way I knew best—as a radio operator in the M.M. (Merchant Marine). I have behind me approximately 2½ years sea-time as a radio operator and now possess a First Class Telegraph License and hold a Lieut. Jr. Grade commission in the U.S. Maritime Service. I either attended school full-time or worked full-time; I could not see part-time school. And besides I could not see any nicer and more interesting way of earning money and seeing so many places. I have crossed the Atlantic 22 times and have traveled by ship some 140,000 miles (nautical). I have seen Paris two times, been to Italy, Portugal, Azores, Norway, Belgium, Venezuela, Colombia, Panama; and up and down the East and West coasts of the U.S., besides hitting some Gulf Ports. I have sailed passenger ships and tankers, but prefer freighters—in fact, Liberties; I know they are slow, but I like the time in port. I have been to Greenland and crossed the Arctic Circle 4 times—but not the equator as yet. So while going through college I worked at the trade that Metro taught me; but now that I have graduated, I am not doing so. The change is because the M.M. as a career is not a desirable one; by that I mean one loses contact with the way of life ashore and soon would become so "salty" that he can never get it out of his blood and as a result could never be happy shoreside; well, I want to be happy because I hope to marry some day and I want to be home with my wife and children! So for awhile the Merchant Marine is a wonderful thing, but to me, not as a career. I do hope to go back for say a year or two to save a nest egg and see the Far East, but then that will be the end. The trouble with Merchant Marine jobs is that there is no shoreside equivalent and therefore one who stays at sea too long and is used to good money finds it hard to return to a poor-paying shoreside job since he is not qualified for much else than to sail a ship. So I have decided to train in a field which will enable me to live shoreside reasonably well.

I am now working for the U.S. Government—Civil Service, as a Radar Instructor for the Signal Corps at Fort Monmouth, New Jersey. I have been here since graduation and have already taught four classes. This change was not unforeseeable; for even during high school I had always felt that I would like to teach; but for two reasons I did not major in education: I could not forsake my major for a lot of repetitious courses in education and I do not want to teach in a high school—I'm afraid my experiences with high schools in general have soured me on that. I have seen so many nice, hard-working teachers bang their heads against the wall that I do not envy them.

I still think we should go on producing Radio Operators. In June 1951 the country was literally crying for Radio Operators to man the ships carrying ECA cargo to Europe and none were to be had. I sailed during that time and I knew the situation and I heard of the fantastic bonuses that were being offered for Radio Operators. The current pay scale for Radio Operators on Liberties is $412 a month with overtime for Saturdays and Sundays at sea; where else can a young fellow have such an opportunity to earn such a good salary and see the world?

In my teaching now I find literally all phases of my studies at Metro useful in teaching GIs Radar repair. At present I am teaching in the Theory of Radar Branch. While at present I suppose I would have to say that I could have done without the Electric Wiring shop, at the time I took it, it would be far from true; for it was the first opportunity I or any student had a chance to work with his hands and to see a few practical applications of electricity in our world.

I believe I am doing very well here at Fort Monmouth. I am, in this short time, doing as well as other instructors who have been there a long time, and in some instances better because of my long experience with radio—and my college training in math and physics which is used rather indirectly as the level of our teaching is geared to high school graduates.

Why is it that the boys of today are not capable of seeing far enough into the future to realize what a singularly wonderful thing is being offered them—free?

Your role as a double-purpose school is a wonderful thing! Had Metropolitan not been available, I would have chosen another school which possessed this duality. Again this is because of the feeling I have that using the hands as well as the brain is the best combination for success. (Moderation in all things, Plato said.)

My shop training at Metro certainly helped me in my lab work in physics. I always liked lab—perhaps sometimes more than theory—especially sometimes when the theory got over my head.

Certainly you may use my name if you publish anything concerning me; in fact it would make me very proud.

Oh yes, I have not finished my formal education. Here at Fort Monmouth, Rutgers University is offering a special three-year course leading to a master's degree in electrical engineering and I am taking it—in fact it was also partially because of this that I came to work here—besides obtaining teaching experience. After I graduate and with my three years of teaching experience I hope to look elsewhere for work; perhaps still in teaching or in industry.

May I humbly apologize for the terrible appearance of this letter; the poor organization and grammatical structure—and worst of all my poor spelling (partly inherent in my nature and partly due to this typewriter). My English courses at college made me quite cognizant of these facts and I am capable—if not rushed—of using them properly. But since you wish this information as quickly as possible and the truth of the matter is that I should be studying for a very important test in Vector Analysis today and tomorrow, I am afraid this is the best I am able to do. Don't think too badly of me.

I sincerely hope that I have been able to help you, Sir, and I wish you all the success with your study.

Edward Corrigan characterizes himself as one of "your ex-problem students." After five terms he left Metropolitan with a good many sad entries on his cumulative record card. But somehow or other, somewhere, sometime, he took hold of himself, and has made an astounding recovery. He not only worked his way through the remainder of high school, but prepared himself for admission to the United States Maritime College. He tells the story:

Upon leaving school I enrolled in the training program sponsored by the Army Transportation Corps. I attended the Transportation Corps Marine School and after my graduation served in various unlicensed capacities aboard Army vessels, for the following two years. After my service with the Army I worked ashore for a short while in fields allied with the marine industry. Eventually, I decided to complete my high school education. This was accomplished by attending classes at the Delehanty High School in Jamaica, New York, where I earned my academic diploma. After acquiring my diploma I submitted an application to take the examinations for the United States Maritime College. After passing the examinations I was appointed to the Academy late in 1950. I have been there since. At present I am engaged in a year's training aboard various vessels of our merchant fleet.

THEY HAVE THEIR OWN DOUBLE PURPOSES

Unless an occupation has become an "educable" profession, pupils in double-purpose schools have difficulty in finding liberal arts colleges where they can continue sound vocational training along with liberal arts subjects. Similarly, the professional schools, especially in the performing arts, have only recently offered the usual "college subjects." The Juilliard School of Music is leading the way in both music and the dance. Bennington is recognizing the dance. Carnegie Tech and Antioch give full play to the drama. But progress is slow. The double-purpose college deserves a book.

Conard Fowkes, son of a Navy man and drama graduate of Performing Arts, compromised with a Navy scholarship at Yale. He is high in his academic grades, but his heart is on the stage. He achieved the dean's list the first year and also played the lead opposite Bibi Osterwald, the Broadway actress, in a Yale production. He showed outstanding talent at Performing Arts and is apparently slated for top roles when Yale and the Navy have had their fling.

As noted in Chapter VI, the School of Performing Arts, a division of Metropolitan Vocational High School, attracts not only pupils with fine talent in the performing arts but those who also rank high in scholastic attainment. Seventy per cent of the graduates go to college. Musicians, actors, dancers, like Conard Fowkes, commandeer as much of their arts as the colleges will allow (often with as much outside instruction as they can pay for), and take "culture" in their stride. In other words, they find that their double-purpose high school has given them thorough-going preparation for college, but that double-purpose colleges are hard to find and, when found, are too expensive to attend.

Irma Pascal found Antioch, which is not only double-purpose in its curriculum but requires students to spend six months of the year in outside occupations. The drama is fostered and practiced and *lived* with the highest enthusiasm. Irma has no double purpose but is letting the drama, as she learned it in high school and exercises it in college, carry her along into absorbing activity. Her reflections throw a white light on the potentialities of occupation centered schools:

If anyone had told me six years ago that I would be attending such a unique high school, in the flick of the eyelash I would have reduced their words to mere dust particles in the air. I was prepared to go to an academic high school and eventually to college. It was the thought of college that spurred me on, not the thought of any high school. Performing Arts is a different thing and was a different thing and excited me with the enthusiasm that is certainly a great part of any high school or college career. The thought of "vocational" held an aura of dirty back rooms and kitchens . . . and sweat shops. So it was with much amazement and reservation that I entered into the venture.

Naturally there are moments in four years of high school, no matter how special a place it is, when one feels doubtful about one's choice. But I never really regretted my choice. I speculate about its wisdom but a pleasant aura hovers about it.

For me, considering the kind of college I chose, it couldn't have been a better high school. Antioch is a small college community in a small town with small town atmosphere. The teachers and the students . . . not only the teachers but the administration *and* faculty manage somehow in five years to establish friendly intimate relationships. Everyone knows everyone else. This has its disadvantages as it did at Performing Arts but in the long run it has more advantages. This was a kind of relationship that I did not have to get used to because of previous training. Since leaving SPA I have talked to a great many students who came from high schools four and five thousand students thick . . . basically most of these people disliked their high schools because they were nothing more than big factories. If Performing Arts' only contribution is to make one feel like a mature, balanced individual whose presence means something more than a written record, then this in itself is a valid enough contribution. But looking back objectively, another great contribution was the variety of interests that it opened up as well as the rich and cultural background it provided for all its students.

For me my drama training just served as a frame of reference for jutting out into writing. The experience has enabled me to take advanced courses in the drama field and do things on an upper class level which as a freshman I ordinarily might not have been able to do. Directing plays last year, writing them, acting a great deal, taking advanced courses, all of this would not have been possible without Performing Arts. If I had not taken Mr. Weiser's course I could never have taken playwriting up here in my first year with all upper class students, and get a grade of A to boot.

If I had not gone to Performing Arts, a summer spent at a Shakespearean festival playing Katherine in *Henry V* would not have been possible because my experience just would not have warranted it. It is true it might have, but I am rather inclined to think it would have been harder.

Now that I am second year I am beginning to be affected more and more by the exciting intellectual and social stimuli here. Without them it might have taken me a longer time to develop into the individual I now am. Performing Arts, because of certain pressures which I will speak of later, tended to make me a much more outgoing person. It tends to train the individual to compete for herself because the atmosphere is so highly competitive.

As for the academic training I can be more specific. The academic training, as such, was as valuable as it would have been in any other high school. The system as it is set up in New York City is neither the best nor the worst. But the criticisms I make are general to all schools and not specific to Performing Arts. That is, after having been here for a year and a half I can honestly say that three-quarters of high school training on an academic level could be thrown out the window. That sounds like pretty strong stuff. I mean it. I can modify it. The regents are of no value, mainly because the courses are designed with regents in mind. In fact the most valuable courses that I got were the courses in which no specific work was being done towards regents. This is a general gripe and may have no value or interest. I am inclined to feel that because Performing Arts has the facilities to offer the unique courses it does and because the student gets so much more than from the average high school, until they abolish regents, "I ain't got no kick coming," to coin a phrase. To evaluate the whole academic program would be impossible. The reasons are all there, but they are hard to express. The only thing that I can say is that it was because of specific teachers and specific academic courses that Performing Arts' academic program stood up. But this was because of a dynamic teaching staff (a part of it) that taught their courses on a college level and in a stimulating way. Another unique thing was the fact that because the classes were small and the group select (aren't all Performing Arts people select?) the classes were conducted on a high intellectual level. Again, I must stress, that this was not only because of the students involved but of the teachers as well. As for sufficient academic background this calls for a treatise. No high school can give it to you. At Antioch or Wellesley or City College you come and learn. And every day you find how much you don't know. College develops your thought processes. Antioch, in particular, because of its unique job program stresses the well-rounded individual, mature, thinking, the person who is developing his thought processes. That is precisely what college does. It introduces a great deal, it pushes the wheels in your head into action. No high school can prepare you for this. Because no high school is equipped. Because of the nature of the high school program the thing it *can* do is to make you feel that you want to learn. That you want to explore. On an academic level as it is set up in a high school this is impossible.

Now, you may think I have gone off the beaten track. I haven't, believe me. Because of this the best possible kind of school is a school like Performing Arts. It is only after having been at college that I realize this. That is, that the practical, as well as cultural training, was the most valuable thing I could derive and that any student can derive. If you are asking is this a success? But yes, Monsieur, it is. . . .

Carolyn Clarke is one of those finely superior persons who would have been outstanding in any type of school. With high intelligence, excellent home environment, and a delightful personality, everything had been in her favor. However, she chose Metropolitan for its opportunities in vocational music and around this core of interest built up an outstanding record in performing skill and in the book subjects. Exhibiting great skill on the French horn, she majored in music in college, graduated with honors, and played with the National Symphony Orchestra. At a later date she writes:

I am still working in that field and have also branched out somewhat. I am still playing the horn professionally and have since taken a year of graduate work at Hunter College in the field of music education, and another year at Boston University, which led to the M.A. degree in Musicology. At present I am a teaching fellow at Boston University and also teaching chamber music at Emmanuel College in Boston. I do some private teaching as well as free-lance work on the horn.

Both the academic studies and the music shop work have been useful to me. If there is a preference, it is probably for the shop work. I could have done without neither type of study.

I am happily married to Leo Panasevich, a member of the Boston Symphony. I look forward eagerly to both a family and a continued part-time music career in teaching and performance.

"THE ARMY IS BREATHING DOWN MY NECK"

The armed forces have already made their influence felt in many of the preceding stories but none of them has been chosen deliberately as an integral part of a complete higher education. Joseph P. Zebrowski, Midshipman 1/c, at the United States Naval Academy, writes his autobiography:

I feel confident that if given the same opportunities in selecting a career I would follow the same pattern of schools. Pulaski Technical High School, University of Maryland two years, U.S. Naval Flight Training Program one year, and the U.S. Naval Academy four years. By attending these different schools I was exposed to varied environments, which I consider an education in itself.

My after school time was spent doing odd chores at the Industrial

Y.M.C.A. for about five years. In shining shoes, running errands for the numberless guests of all types, I was able to decide definitely what I wanted from life. I became determined that I was going to get a college education, preferably an engineering one, as I liked mathematics and engineering methods.

After graduation from grammar school I chose Pulaski Technical because I wanted to be an engineer, preferably civil, so that I could do something creative. I did not realize then that the cultural courses like history, language, literature, which were stressed in the high school, were of any significance; and consequently had no desire of going there; furthermore I knew that I could be admitted to almost every college in the country. This was indeed very encouraging as I did want to attend the better known schools. The only shortcoming that one attending a technical school has is in his background of cultural subjects; and I sincerely believe that this can be included without sacrificing the technical training.

During my high school period I also cultivated an interest for both service academies, showing partiality toward the Naval Academy. There were many seamen that came to the "Y" and that perhaps explains the reason. I made my desires known to a couple of politicians and after waiting several weeks got the usual reply of "no vacancies." I then abandoned the thought, temporarily.

At the completion of high school, 1946, we had wonderful opportunities of entering an Army or Navy program. I took and passed exams for the Naval Aviation College Program. Through this program I obtained two years at the University of Maryland in the engineering course. At the end of these two years, I had the option of staying at the University of Maryland or reporting to Pensacola for flight duty. I chose the latter, as I always admired, and still do, the Navy pilots. They were an outfit that I wanted to be a part of. This was my first major decision by going to Pensacola and I did it with this in mind: "Never feel sorry for what you do—think before you do it."

While at Pensacola, my spark for the Naval Academy regenerated itself after talking to some alumni. I immediately proceeded to obtain an appointment, and while flying I received notice to report to the Naval Academy. I had successfully completed 70 hours, 45 hours dual instruction and 25 hours solo, and I loved flying.

I felt that this was my only opportunity and if not taken, I might regret the decision for the rest of my days. I made my second decision with the knowledge that I will have the best training for the profession that I choose, and with the hope that I will be able to continue flying after graduation. I do not regret this decision, because when reminiscing about the year spent here, I feel a sense of accomplishment which I did not realize before.

In June, 1953, I will obtain my sheepskin, which I shall cherish for many a day. This in a sense is only the beginning of my learning, as it will continue for as long as I'm in the Navy. I feel confident that with my background I will be able to discharge my duties competently.

FROM SHOP TO COLLEGE

Printing, sheet metal, and office practice do not immediately suggest college, but that unusual association is the fascinating educational implication of the double-purpose school. Out of the shops and offices comes the broad-gauge man or woman. The principals of San Antonio and Gerstmeyer (Terre Haute) Technical High Schools tell significant stories:

Frank Williams, son of C. P. Williams—founder of the Sheet Metal Shop in the San Antonio Vocational and Technical School—enrolled in his daddy's course in the Fall of 1945. A leader in every respect, Frank concluded his senior high school career by winning a scholarship for having the highest grades in his class. His record was, with one exception (a single grade of B), a straight A report. As a result of his scholastic attainment, he received the scholarship awarded annually to the highest ranking graduate. But that is only part of the story. He served as president of his Sophomore, Junior and Senior classes; was elected to the National Honor Society; won an American Legion oratorical contest; and was an active member of the Student Council, the Glee Club, the Tech Little Theatre, and the Press Club. Frank completed the Smith-Hughes Vocational Sheet Metal course along with enough college entrance subjects to enable him to enter college.

After two years of college, he deferred additional training in order to support his wife and baby. At the present time he is working in a sheet metal shop in San Antonio and is drawing top union wages.

In January 1948, a quiet, soft-spoken, brown-eyed, curly haired boy (Albert Villarreal) enrolled in the Tech Print Shop. Very shortly thereafter, the printing teacher remarked to the journalism teacher across the hall, "I think we've got a fine boy among our new students." The prediction was accurate because two years later this boy, as an all-round editor-printer, was able to get a news story, write it up, edit it, write the headline, then set the type, read the proof, make the corrections, make up the form, and run the paper on the press.

In spite of this full-time, double-duty job, Albert found time to belong to the Tech Press Club, and the Alamo Press Association. He served as reporter for the Student Council and his Senior Class.

His good grades won him his election to the National Honor Society and to Quill and Scroll, which is an international honorary society for high school journalists. The *Technician*, school paper, which he edited, won state, national, and international honors.

Upon completing his vocational printing course and graduating from high school, Albert was awarded a one-year scholarship to St. Mary's University of San Antonio. He is now both a college student and a printer. His major subjects are English and Journalism, and the minute that he is through with classes each day, he reports to a local newspaper office where, as linotype operator, he is earning the money for completion of his college course.

George C. entered the Gerstmeyer Technical High School because it offered extensive vocational work. After one year of tryout in the wood shop, he found that he had no talent for woodworking but was interested in tool room organization; so he changed to the commercial course.

After graduating from Gerstmeyer, George entered the School of Commerce at Indiana University. He was an outstanding member of track teams in both high school and college.

During World War II, George became a pilot with the rank of first lieutenant. While in India, he organized and took charge of technical equipment. After the war was over, he remained in the service for a year. At Williams Field in Chandler, Arizona, he was assigned the task of reorganizing the technical shops. After being released from the service, he returned to Indiana University and completed the Bachelor's and Master's degrees in the School of Commerce.

His first position was in personnel work with one of the leading national bakeries but George was not happy in this work. Today, he is with one of the major appliance companies as a commercial engineer.

Since the Gerstmeyer Technical High School offers both vocational and academic work, George C. received a well-rounded education. He not only acquired the know-how to earn his present position as commercial engineer with one of the major appliance companies, but moreover, he developed the qualifications that make him a valuable citizen in his community.

George's experiences in leadership, athletics, and speech work in Gerstmeyer contribute to his ability to participate in the Junior Chamber of Commerce and the Toastmasters' Club in Richmond, Indiana, where he lives with his wife and son.

THEY LIKED TEACHING

Out of double-purpose schools come teachers of vocational and technical subjects. Gerstmeyer (Terre Haute) and Joliet Township High Schools provide important instances:

John V. withdrew from one high school in Terre Haute, Indiana, to enroll in the Gerstmeyer Technical High School for vocational and technical training. While enrolled in Gerstmeyer, he became interested in printing and made this subject his vocational major. During his junior and senior years, he worked in a print shop on the cooperative school and shop training program.

He graduated from high school in 1928 and worked as an apprentice in a print shop for one year. He then decided he would like to become a printing teacher. He enrolled in Indiana State Teachers College in 1929 and majored in Industrial Arts, specializing in printing. He received the B.S. degree in 1933. Unable to get a teaching job, he worked in a print shop until 1936, at which time he secured a position with the Terre Haute Public Schools as printing instructor at the Gerstmeyer Technical High School.

During the summers of 1937 and 1938, John enrolled as an advanced printing student at the Carnegie Institute of Technology. He received the M.S. degree in Education in 1949.

At the present time, he is head of the printing department and manager of athletics at the Gerstmeyer Technical High School.

John is a member of the American Vocational Association, Indiana Industrial Education Association, Indiana Vocational Education Association, Phi Delta Kappa, International Typographical Union, Indiana State Teachers Association, and American Federation of Teachers.

Bernard Leighton Wellman was born in Joliet, Illinois, June 27, 1908. He attended Joliet Grade School, and came to Joliet Township High School in September, 1922. His high school courses included work in both the academic and the vocational schools.

His record was outstanding, and he earned one of the highest averages ever recorded here. He won the Adam Award for scholarship and outstanding achievement when he graduated in 1926.

He enrolled in the Engineering Course in Junior College in the Fall term, 1926, and made an immediate impression upon all of his teachers. He went right on making high grades and showed himself to be well able to carry engineering work on a high level.

After two years in Junior College he went to the University of Illinois, on the Rotary Club scholarship, and graduated in Mechanical Engineering in 1930. Upon graduation he entered Worcester Polytechnic Institute as an instructor in Mechanical Drawing where his immediate success paralleled his work done in college.

He has written one of the outstanding Descriptive Geometry textbooks, and is now a full professor of Mechanical Engineering at Worcester Polytechnic Institute.

Art and Life and Education

It is not only in "profiles" or "closeups" that occupations, professions, jobs, and careers attain to literary stature. Fiction, drama, poetry are arts that capture the desire of man to work and live. As Irwin Edman says,[2] "Whatever life may be, it is an experience.

[2] Irwin Edman, *Arts and the Man*, New York, Mentor Books, 1951.

Whatever experience may be, it is a flow through time, a duration, a many-colored episode in eternity. Wherever materials are given form, wherever movement is given direction, wherever life has line and composition, there we have intelligence, there we have that transformation of a given chaos into a desired and desirable order that we call Art. . . . The Arts are absorbing flights from life, but they may—in major instances, they do—*clarify, intensify,* and *interpret* life."

If these stories we have just told were "transformed into a desired and desirable order," they would be art. In very fact, except for the eternal triangle, the interest of drama and fiction center upon the tragedy or felicity of an occupation—two of the latest are *Death of a Salesman* and *Point of No Return.* Then there were *Golden Boy,* the Horatio Alger boys, Captain Ahab, all the doctor, lawyer, and minister books, and Jarndyce and Jarndyce in Dickens' *Bleak House.* In *The Man of the House* Frank O'Connor wrote: "As a kid I was as good as gold so long as I could concentrate. Concentration, that was always my trouble, in school and everywhere else. Once I was interrupted I was lost." His mother got sick, was doubled with pain, but wanted to do her usual housework. " 'You shouldn't work like that,' I said, 'go on up to bed and I'll bring you your breakfast.' It's a funny thing about women, the way they'll take orders from anything in trousers, even if 'tis only ten." So the "kid" became the man of the house.

Our boys and girls become men and women, not only of the house, but of the world at large.

THE TRUTH OF THE MATTER

Insistently, seemingly repetitiously, we have laid stress upon the differences among young people. Parents often complain that their own children, born of the same parents, are "as different as day and night." In schools the differences are compounded by race, religion, wealth, poverty, status. Yet the youngsters are taught the same subjects by the same teachers. What to do about it?

First, as we have also insistently and repeatedly stressed, the school must offer every possible different kind of opportunity for learning. "Double-purpose" is only a convenient relative term—triple, quadruple, multipurpose, would be better.

Second, no one can learn *anything* for which his previous *experience* has not given him prehensile claws. Learning is experience piled up on experience, and experience is doing *doing,* DOING.

Third, experience must be purposeful and guided. The undertones and overtones of our profiles are a continuous expression of gratitude to teachers and counselors, men and women who have piloted their young through devious and confusing channels. No school, single or multipurpose, can educate without the deeply interested, wholly dedicated members of the staff. Both the organization and personnel must be gaited to the vibrant youth who are trying to find their way.

Fourth, and primarily, the parents, the board of education members, the citizens, must know what is going on in the school community. They must see, hear, and feel what their own and their neighbors' children are doing seven or eight hours every day (homework included!).

Some of us read with considerable interest that most literate of daily columns, "Topics of the Times." Recently the writer wrestled with a school problem.

Hope springs eternal in the breasts of parents on a good many subjects, and one of them is the matter of child-to-parent communication. Each autumn about this time parents hope that this year things will be different, that this year the child will come home when the school day is over to discuss freely and at length news of the classroom. Last autumn, and the autumn before that—and possibly even further back—the pattern was the same. The pupil would come home from school to deposit his books before disappearing until dinner time and he would be asked one of the several possible variations of the question, "How was school today?"—in a voice carefully relaxed, containing no hint of anxiety or undue curiosity—and he would reply in one of the several possible variations of "It was okay."

The writer goes on to deplore the number of untoward incidents and towardly events blanketed under "It was okay"—a water pistol fray, appointment to a safety patrol squad, dreadful failures in arithmetic, undelivered announcements from the parent-teacher association. Then:

> Report cards make their way through too. Then it may turn out how inadequate "It was okay" has been as a report on the school day. The mark in the square next to "Deportment" may suggest that while this pupil was saying, so nonchalantly, "It was okay," he was the ringleader of a plot to undermine discipline throughout the school system. What did he do to deserve a next-to-nothing mark in deportment? "Nothing special" will be the reply.
>
> But perhaps this year will be better. Perhaps one day this week the returning student will say of his day, "It was pretty good," or "It was a bad day; I got a 'D' in spelling," instead of "It was okay," and if that happens, progress will have been made.

The *New York Times* reporter is like too many other parents—loving, trusting, suspecting, hopeful, but not school-visiting. Under bland indifference he senses trouble that he doesn't find. The teachers and the parents must know each other better so that all of them may really discover what kind of children they are fussing with.

They will know who these boys and girls are, and when they query, "How was school today," they'll be able to answer for themselves that "It was okay."

VIII. Utopia

Toward more useful curricula

For some time American education has shown a strong tendency —in theory—to provide flexible curricula with which to meet differentiated individual needs, as well as the complex social demands of the community. This study has shown where and how these needs and demands have actually been met—in practice. In the preceding two chapters we have presented firsthand accounts of a dozen double-purpose schools which appear to have shown the way and of many of their students who have found the way.

UTOPIA IN AMERICAN CITY

Also illuminating is the hypothetical "American City" located in the equally mythical "State of Columbia" which was described in *Education for All American Youth*, published in 1944 by the Educational Policies Commission of the National Education Association of the United States and the American Association of School Administrators. The plan for this "American City" of about 150,000 population (plus 20,000 more in the nearby territory) generally calls for three high schools besides the community institute which provides completion of high school work and a variety of daytime and evening classes for adults. It goes without saying that it is much easier to put the content of these proposals down on paper than it is to offer them in an actual city school system. To express it in extreme form, if one boy in a thousand needs a particular subject, who will teach it—where and when—and who will pay the cost of providing virtually a private tutor? These are organizational problems that try the souls of earnest, seeking educators.

However, the "American City" plan of the Educational Policies Commission is indicative of the kind of thinking that stimulates action and, taken in conjunction with what already has actually been done, can be of the greatest usefulness. The emphasis of the "American City" plan is upon flexibility and adaptability and milieu. The following statement and chart (p. 159) explain the curricula:

Numbers, however, are not nearly so important as what youth learn in these schools. When we inquire into that, the most striking fact which we meet is that each of the three high schools and the community institute endeavors to meet all of the "imperative educational needs of youth."

Whichever school a student may attend, he will find a balanced program, designed to help him grow in occupational proficiency; in competence as a citizen; in satisfying relationships in family, school, and other personal associations; in health and physical fitness; in discriminating expenditure of money and of time; in enjoyable and constructive use of leisure; and in understanding and appreciation of his cultural heritage.

The staff of each school first of all endeavors to know its students as individuals. This is fundamental to program planning and to teaching. For while the general needs of youth are common to all, the specific needs of each individual are in some respects unique.

The curriculum of each school includes four divisions of learning, designated as "Vocational Preparation," "Individual Interests," "Common Learnings," and "Health and Physical Education." In addition, there is a tenth-grade course on science, closely related to the course on "Common Learnings." The first two divisions are referred to as the "area of differential studies" since students elect their programs in these fields from a variety of offerings. The last two divisions and the science course are called "the area of common studies" since here all students follow the same general programs. Each student normally divides his time between these two divisions.

The content of each of these divisions is summarized on the chart. . . . One point, however, should be underlined, in order to avoid possible confusion. The work in "Vocational Preparation" may be either (1) study, practice, and work experience, intended to equip a youth to go directly to work from high school or community institute, or (2) the study of sciences, mathematics, foreign languages, and other subjects which are part of the equipment for advanced study in the community institute, a four-year college, or a university.

For a student following the usual schedule, vocational preparation will occupy one-sixth of his school time in Grade X, one-third in Grades XI and XII, one-half in community institute. On "Common Learnings," he will spend one-third of his time in each year of high school, one-sixth in community institute. Science will occupy one-sixth of his time in Grade X. One-sixth of his time will be given to health and physical education throughout the five years and the same to "Individual Interests." Formularized though this curricula may seem, it still has its provisions for flexibility:

At first sight, this schedule may seem to be rigid and unyielding— ill suited to the purpose of serving youth according to their needs. But that is by no means the case. In practice this curriculum is sufficiently flexible to permit almost any student to follow a program "tailor-made" to his needs.

Take first the possible adaptations in the schedule itself. Suppose a student is not ready to make even a tentative choice of an occupational field in tenth grade. He is not required to do so and may elect two courses, instead of one, in a field of avocational, cultural, or intellectual interest. Suppose, on the other hand, that a twelfth-grade student needs more than two periods a day for machine-shop practice and related training, to get ready for a job which is awaiting him. He may use the individual-interests period for additional vocational education.

Suppose that a student has a strong interest in aeronautical engineering and wants to go to a university school of engineering immediately after twelfth grade. In his vocational preparation time, he can study physics, chemistry, and three years of mathematics; and he may use his individual-interest time, if he so desires, for as many as three more courses related to his major interest. Or, take the case

Periods per day (average for the year)	Grades	High School			Community Institute	
		X	XI	XII	XIII	XIV

1

Individual Interests

(Elected by the student, under guidance, in fields of avocational, cultural, or intellectual interest.) — — — — — — — — — — — — — — — — — — *

2

Vocational Preparation

(Includes education for industrial, commercial, home-making, service, and other occupations leading to employment, apprenticeship, or homemaking at the end of Grade XII, XIII, or XIV; education for technical and semiprofessional occupations in community institute; and the study of sciences, mathematics, social studies, literature, and foreign languages in preparation for advanced study in community institute, college, or university. May include a period of productive work under employment conditions, supervised by the school staff. Related to the study of economics and industrial and labor relations in "Common Learnings.")

3

Science

(Methods, principles, and facts needed by all students.)

4

Common Learnings

(A continuous course for all, planned to help students grow in competence as citizens of the community and the nation; in understanding of economic processes and of their roles as producers and

5

consumers; in cooperative living family, school, and community; in appreciation of literature and the arts; and in use of the English language. Guidance of individual students is a chief responsibility of "Common Learnings" teachers.)

**

6

Health and Physical Education

(Includes instruction in personal health and hygiene; health examinations and follow-up; games, sports, and other activities to promote physical fitness. Related to study of community health in "Common Learnings.")

* Broken line indicates flexibility of scheduling.
** Solid line marks the division between "differential studies" (above) and "common studies" (below).

of a community-institute student who is already reasonably well prepared for employment or for home-making, but wants to learn more about history, economics, literature, or the arts. It is possible for this student to spend two or three periods a day on these interests, instead of one, with corresponding reduction in time for vocational preparation.

More important than flexibility of scheduling is flexibility of class instruction. One result of the long process of cooperative planning is that teachers throughout the American City schools now endeavor to suit learning experiences within classes to the abilities and needs of individual students.

And what is the community institute, which plays so important a part in the "American City"?

Here is a new institution, only four years old, yet already enrolling nearly 4,000 students. It was established because the people responsible for educational planning in American City and in the state of Columbia came to the conclusion that a large proportion of youth needed free public education beyond the twelfth grade, chiefly to prepare them for occupations which require training beyond that which is possible in high school, and also to carry them forward in the general education appropriate to free men in American democracy. That these people judged rightly is shown by the school's enrollment.

PERSPECTIVE OF THE PRESIDENT'S COMMISSION

Even more tangible than the Educational Policies Commission's plan for the future are the findings of the President's Commission on Higher Education. Since the commission was asked by the President of the United States to focus its activities on long-range policies, it arbitrarily set the date 1960 as its target, "since it was felt that manageable data could be procured for studies up to this point."

By 1960, therefore, the commission believes that "a minimum of 4,600,000 young people should be enrolled in nonprofit institutions for education beyond the traditional twelfth grade. Of this total number, 2,500,000 should be in the thirteenth and fourteenth (junior college level), 1,500,000 in the fifteenth and sixteenth grades (senior college level), and 600,000 in graduate and professional schools beyond the first degree.

Although the commission recognized that it was in no position to "predict annual enrollments over the period 1948 to 1960," it instead "staked out what it believes to be the desirable goal in terms of the number of young people that higher education should serve." To help find this goal in terms of numbers, the commission evolved what it termed its "National Inventory of Talent," which revealed that:

1—At least 49 percent of our population has the mental ability to complete 14 years of schooling with a curriculum of general and vocational studies that should lead either to gainful employment or to further study at a more advanced level.

2—At least 32 percent of our population has the mental ability to complete an advanced liberal or specialized professional education.

In line with its over-all aim to outline the possibilities for the best possible education for the most possible persons, the President's Commission (in Volume I of its report, published in 1947) commented as follows on the interrelationship of general and vocational education:

Although general education, as the term is currently used, is concerned with the nonspecialized activities of living, it is by no means antagonistic to vocational education. Rightly conceived, the two are complementary. General education should contribute to vocational competence by providing the breadth of view and perspective that make the individual a more effective worker and a more intelligent member of a society of freemen.

It is urgently important in American education today that the age-old distinction between education for living and education for making a living be discarded.

The idea has long prevailed in our tradition, and it is still prevalent today, that a liberal education is one thing and professional or vocational education is another, that the two should be sharply differentiated, that one is preparation for labor, the other for leisure. Some go so far as to reject vocational education entirely calling it "servile" and to disclaim for liberal education any intention to be useful. Others, admitting the need for both general and special education, still seek to keep them apart in the curricula. They hold that during a certain period of one's formal education one should pursue the ends of a liberal general education exclusively and then, if interested in a vocation or profession, that with even greater singularity of purpose.

Much of present-day educational theory and practice is based on this fundamental misconception of the relationship between liberal and vocational education. The fact is that education is a unified process, developing in the student the qualities of mind and personality required of him both for making a living and for building a life.

The idea that vocational education is "servile" is certainly long since out-of-date. By broadening the basis of government to include all the people, democracy has made it necessary to give to all citizens the education formerly reserved for a privileged class. There can no longer be a distinction between inferiors trained only for practical tasks and superiors trained for government or the professions. Democratic society does not support a leisure class of gentlemen, nor does it distinguish between citizens and workers. Making a living is a function of the citizen and being a citizen is a function of the worker.

To build a richly textured and gracious life is a good and desirable purpose, but few of us can make such a life without first making a living. Cultural values soon take wing when men cannot get and hold jobs.

The President's Commission clearly reported in favor of a unification of educational objectives and processes which would "provide, at appropriate levels, proper combinations of general and special education for students of varying abilities and occupational objectives." About vocational education the commission stated:

Vocational or professional training is essential in our industrial society. It is essential from the viewpoint of the individual who must support himself and his family. Special training is already highly important in the competition for good jobs and for advancement in one's chosen vocation, and the chances are that it will become more so.

Vocational education is necessary, too, from the viewpoint of State and the Nation. Society has a great deal of work of many kinds to be done, if the social organization is to function smoothly and move forward to higher levels of good living. And society looks to the schools to provide the trained personnel for all its vast, complex activities. Institutions of higher education must assume their full share of responsibility for providing a sufficient number of qualified persons in all fields to satisfy the demands of society.

Noting the profound changes which the complexity of modern technological society has brought about in the economic system of old rural America, the President's Commission commented on the contribution of the land-grant colleges and the full challenge which the new order brings to all higher education:

The land-grant colleges have been a potent factor in the democratization of higher education; they have brought it to the service of the practical affairs of life and of all classes, trades, and professions; they have given dignity to many occupations in both agriculture and industry. Through research and teaching, they have contributed immensely to the increased productivity of farm labor, and through their programs of home economics and their extension service they have enriched the quality of rural life. Their efforts in all these directions should be extended.

The purpose of the land-grant colleges and of higher education generally should be to prepare many young people, including some farm youth, for effective living in a new industrial and urban environment, and to give youth who will remain on the farm both the broad general education and the vocational training they will require for a better command over the physical and human resources of their environment.

IX. Toward Teaching the Whole Man

What to do about the high schools?

The inescapable fact about people is their diversity. The depressing truth about curricula is their uniformity. A curriculum is a course to be run—by the fleet-footed, by the lame, the well, the sick, the bright, the dull, the intellectual, the athletic—and the well-educated are those who finish on time.

Schoolmen believe in the individual; they exalt him; but—he must run his course. If he takes too long or quits the race, he is a poor student or a drop-out. Teachers, counselors, administrators give him good advice. They help him along. They may even change his course. But speaking generally, he must finish to win.

Now recognition of the individual, respect for personality, carries with it the obligation of educating that human being in terms of his own nature as well as of the composite nature of two billion other human beings. Therefore, fundamental and precedent to the educational process itself is a determination of what that education should be. This is not a single act, but a series of evaluations or reevaluations. It is a guidance program. Such a program is not merely a diagnosis of the individual. It is, in the final analysis, an evolution of education itself.[1]

Emphasis has been laid in the preceding pages upon the concept that "vocational education is not job training merely." It is many, many other things. As has also been said, "It merely touches off a spark, it releases latent energy. It gives the living a chance to live." It is what general education would be if it were as general

[1] Franklin J. Keller, *Principles of Vocational Education*, Boston, D. C. Heath and Company, 1948, p. 69.

and as specific as it should be. And this study is an approach to a formula that would meet the needs of *all* the people. Expert knowledge, expert skill, *is* the ground to start from. The road traveled and the goal reached depend upon the individual and the kind of society in which he finds himself.

After a study of the kinds of secondary schools that are available for our young people, we draw certain conclusions as to effectiveness and make a number of recommendations as to what secondary education should provide. Our conception of vocational education is different from that often found in educational literature. It is a whole, comprehensive, all-inclusive education for boy or girl. Vocational education is not merely the giving of a scrap of knowledge or the giving of expertness in a manual operation. It is the teaching of the whole man in the life situation in which he finds himself, or to which he aspires. This distinction is of the utmost importance.

While our conclusions are bound to range over the whole field of secondary education, *the findings of this particular study relate only to those high school pupils who, through intellectual and manual interests and abilities, are fitted to prepare for both vocation and college entrance.* Problems of the gifted child, the slow learner, the comprehensive high school, and the like are contemplated as subjects of future research.

TIME AND CONTENT IN SECONDARY SCHOOLS

In terms of time and content the generally established forty-period vocational high school schedule offers potentially 33⅓ to 40 percent more education than does the generally accepted academic high school. The vocational high school has a 6-hour day and a 30-hour week, whereas the academic high school has a 5- or 5¼-hour day and a 25- or 26-hour week. Moreover, within these 25 hours there are usually only 25 to 30 45-minute periods. That is to say, the academic high school student has a number of free or study periods, whereas the vocational high school student is under instruction every one of the forty periods that he attends school. He has no free or study periods. In some respects, the vocational high school pupil may be represented as taking the same program as his contemporary in an industrial arts course in a general high school plus 15 additional periods of shop work.

This simple statement of a statistical fact is of the utmost importance. It is tantamount to saying that the academic high school fails to use at least 33⅓ percent of every pupil's optimum time for education, and that, by doing so, it could provide this education by giving a full day's work in a school equipped to handle the occupational phases. In effect it challenges the academic school with the task of providing the indispensable vocational features of sound education by utilizing the already available school time for both occupational and academic instruction instead of providing only for the verbal aspects of life.

This study indicates, without question, that, within a reasonably long (or reasonably short, according to the point of view) period, the American secondary school can give an entirely adequate education for adolescents, including thoroughgoing vocational education and guidance. There are now enough schools in the United States, in enough different kinds of economic and social communities, to serve as outstanding evidence of the possibility of such a diversified, yet well integrated education.

Too Much Emphasis on "Time Spent in School"?

Several critics who read our original manuscript have taken exception to the bald statement: "In terms of *time* and *content* the generally established forty-period vocational school *offers potentially 33⅓ to 40 percent more education* than does the *generally accepted* academic high school." One notes: "It is quite possible that students in some vocational high schools have few opportunities for using the library, for participation in school activities and for developing needed social skills. If so, an entirely contrary conclusion might be justified." Another argues: [As I understand it] "this conclusion is based upon the assumption that when pupils in academic schools use part of their school time in study periods, they are not engaging in educational activities. This conclusion is questionable. Also it might be argued that inasmuch as academic pupils are commonly given many more homework assignments than are vocational pupils, they are actually spending more hours than are pupils in vocational schools."

A third educator comments: [The paragraph containing this statement] "confused me for awhile, and I think it would probably antagonize some readers who would otherwise be sympathetic with the development of your thesis. I presume that you introduced this statement in order to follow the newspaper style of stating the most important things at the very beginning of an article. I believe that, in general, however, this paragraph could be just as effective if you worked up to it gradually. I have not read every page as carefully as I should like, but I still fail to find the basic data on which this conclusion is apparently based."

Three more schoolmen express their doubts: "I doubt that you could substantiate that statement except in terms of time spent in school, but when put on the basis of education acquired, it becomes difficult to prove." "There is tremendous emphasis on the length of the school day. I wonder whether more emphasis should not be placed on what is done with the school day than on the hours *per se*." "Study periods are necessary to a good education if properly used. The vocational schools described must surely require a lot of evening homework not so necessary in academic high schools because of opportunities provided *in* school. Sometimes students need to *escape from* constant instruction in order to learn. It is not what students are 'taught' but what they 'learn' that counts. No one can be given an education—he must work for it—earn it. And some of it must be done by himself! Insofar as *day length* is concerned, with academic and vocational students, both working efficiently approximately the same number of hours, it may be assumed they are benefiting somewhat equally (that is, fully) although along different lines with different outcomes. This must be clarified to prove that the vocational schools give one-third more education than academic schools."

These are well-considered comments by keenly intelligent and highly responsible educators. Therefore, let us note that:

(1) Throughout the revision of the manuscript we have striven to clarify the results of our study. We have emphasized "time" over quality of content with the thought that it is the prime requisite *in school* for the offering of any kind of education.

(2) It is important to mark carefully in our statement the key words: *in terms of time, offers potentially, and generally accepted.*

(3) While we have made no study of *"quality of content"* (we hope to do so later), we do offer considerable detailed information regarding what is actually taught in a number of schools where a full thirty-hour week is devoted to teaching, both vocational and general. The reality of intention (and probable accomplishment) in certain "double-purpose" secondary schools, and the potentiality in all other schools, are the salient points in the present study.

(4) On the basis of our knowledge of these double-purpose schools, it is a fair assumption that they do (certainly can) provide time for use of library, participation in school activities, development of needed social skills, and the like, just as effectively as the accepted academic school. In fact, the vocational element in the curricula is likely to make these activities ever so much more vital.

(5) In a double-purpose school there will be (at least can be) just as much homework as in an academic school. Whether this "homework" can be done more effectively in school in a "study

period" is a moot point. If it can, there is always the possibility of extending the school day. Probably the most important question is, however, whether the average secondary school does enough educationally profitable "work" at an age when the normal seven- or eight-hour day should be fully and earnestly occupied (another problem for research).

THE VOCATIONAL HIGH SCHOOL AND THE COMPREHENSIVE HIGH SCHOOL

The comprehensive high school is often discussed on the assumption that it is a clearly defined and going institution. As a matter of fact, it is never (perhaps never can be) as comprehensive as its name suggests. It should be all things to all young men and women. It is a place where they can get just the kind of education that each one wants and needs. It provides (as all the academic authorities agree it should) full preparation for occupational as well as other phases of life. It should offer occupational training that is really "vocational." The time given should be wholly adequate. The number of pupils assigned to vocational work should be comparable to the number actually capable of performing it rather than consist almost entirely of those who have been unsuccessful in academic work and have been thrown into "vocational work" as a last resort. Fortunately, a few schools, as indicated in Chapter VI and described in brief summary below, have tackled this problem with a view to providing young people with a broad preparation for life (including both the so-called vocational and academic phases) and some of them have had considerable success.

As pointed out in *Education for All American Youth*, any schedule set down on paper is likely to seem rigid and unyielding—ill suited to the purpose of serving youth according to their needs. However, the curriculum must be sufficiently flexible to permit almost any student to follow a program tailored to his needs. It is also pointed out that the pupil must find "a balanced program, designed to help him grow in occupational proficiency; in competence as a citizen; in satisfying relationships in family, school, and other personal associations, in health and physical fitness; in discriminating expenditure of money, and of time; in enjoyable and constructive use of leisure; and in understanding and appreciation of his cultural heritage."

WHAT ABOUT VOCATIONAL GUIDANCE?

"Flexibility," "diversification," and "orientation" are all key words in any educational program. Therefore, several of our critics deplore the absence of stress upon guidance. And well they may, for it is of primary importance. It is a *sine qua non*. Yet, like the education of the pupil who cannot profit from the college preparatory course, it is a problem which, though germane to our main thesis, is not a subject in our immediate task. It is not stressed; indeed is only mentioned. Meanwhile, so that there may be no misconception of the fundamental and vital place it takes in our thinking, we refer to the opening words in this chapter, and to the chapter on "Vocational High School Teachers, Guidance Counselors, and Advisory Committees" in *Education for an Industrial Age*.[2]

WHAT ABOUT MENTAL HEALTH?

It has been suggested that such a book as this, on education and schools, should contain some reference to mental health. That subject will doubtless receive special attention in one or another of the prospective Barney Project studies. Its omission from the body of the book is more apparent than real, though the term is not used. What we may emphasize here is that mental

[2] Alfred Kahler and Ernest Hamburger, *Education for an Industrial Age*, Ithaca and New York, Cornell University Press, 1948. Sponsored by the Edgar Starr Barney Project.

health values are *implicit* in the kind of education with which the following pages deal, and in its methods of preparation for, through present participation in, not only the world of occupations but life in an occupational world. The relation of doing, work, and occupation to the educative process and the development of personality has long been recognized; and in education as we conceive it are to be found many of the prime requisites for positive mental health—purposeful activity, tied in with the fulfilment of individual powers and capacities, along with the socialized experience of work and occupation, all leading to a sense both of personal competence and of social usefulness. For there is a good deal more in mental health education than goes by that name, and more in mental health and progressive maturity than is, or can be, taught as a classroom subject; to a large extent mental health is a by-product of successful doing and living and of appropriate education thereof. Moreover, while specialized mental hygiene facilities and services in the schools are needful, particularly but not solely for problem cases, it should be stressed that the classroom teacher and the personal or vocational counselor, in their own daily work, can greatly help their charges in many instances of emotional difficulty by sympathetic understanding and by understanding advice.

VOCATIONAL SCHOOLS AND COLLEGE PREPARATION

Vocational and technical high schools can and do offer college preparatory work in connection with their vocational courses. Our study reveals carefully devised secondary school programs and thoughtful special programming of individual pupils. The schools we have studied are going institutions regularly and adequately preparing pupils for both the occupational and cultural demands of life.

Can vocational preparation abide with college preparation? Despite the evidence offered by the foregoing schools some of our critics think the two kinds of preparation just cannot live together or that they may lead unhappy lives. One of our friends comments: "Why should a given pupil who starts his secondary education with the avowed purpose of preparing for college, and evidence of likelihood of realizing his ambition, be expected to take a heavy vocational program for a less-than-college objective along with a college preparatory program? To be sure, it is very creditable to a vocational school that it gives inspiration for higher education to a pupil who started with other than college aspirations, and its varied program should be liberally accepted by the college for admission."

We express no conviction as to what courses *all* secondary pupils should take, but rather the belief that all pupils should have the opportunity to combine vocational and college preparatory courses whenever their interests and sound guidance procedures indicate the desirability. We present evidence of the possibility of doing this effectively.

Another critic states: "As we understand your presentation, you have as your problem the comparative study of the curricula of vocational and academic high schools in larger units of population, and you claim that since a few schools are making a success of an integrated program by half-time on vocational and half-time on academic work, this hybrid is the most successful approach to the problem. . . . You are promoting a school-focusing pupil-interest in the prospective vocation for approximately half the school day and in the academic, college preparatory subjects for the other half. Our opinion is that this is integration in its worst form and should be resisted as the emasculation of vocational education."

A third critic writes: "My own personal philosophy would not be in accord with your plan. . . . Frankly, it appears that your motto is 'A college degree in every pocket!' We believe the motto should be 'A happy and well-trained worker on every job!' . . .

I do believe more reports of this type should be written. Without them it is impossible for there to be a great deal of progress made in vocational education."

Again, may we say that we advocate this program only for those who want it and can take it, and that we have no motto except that every youth should have an adequate and appropriate education.

"Work Experience," Diversified Occupations, and the Split Program

"Work experience" has recently become a familiar phrase among academic school men. Much has been said about the superior quality of work experience as an educational measure. This is often equivalent to saying that schools are not much good when it comes to preparing for occupational life; that they are only good for teaching those things for which "life experience" is not sufficient. In fact, it is true that the schools are now trying to teach many things that used to be learned in the family and in the community through "experience." Even the three R's sometimes come off badly. Of course, any oversimplification of this kind is invalid, but it does call attention to the fact that "work experience" is not an easy answer to the problem of vocational preparation.

Nevertheless, many schools, especially in small communities where specific instruction in a number of different trades would be difficult to give in school, have met the situation by allowing upper-grade pupils to work part of their school time in the various stores and industries of the town and have designated coordinators to tally up the work experience with school learning.

In at least three cities, high school seniors are permitted to spend half of each day in their home school and the other half in the city's vocational high school, taking two subjects in the home school and three hours of vocational work in the vocational high school. A similar practice existed in New York City during the years of World War II. This is a good example of "program flexibility." It is probably an attempt to carry out by indirection, a practice that ought to be boldly included in the basic organization of the schools. In any case, it is evident, whether occupational and cultural education are given in the same schools, or in different schools, or in school and in life situations, the method and means of uniting them in a "whole education" are many and various, but they can all be practical.

VOCATIONAL COURSES IN RELATION TO COLLEGE ADMISSION

There is a slow but definite trend toward the crediting of vocational courses for admission to college. Twenty-eight state universities grant from one to six credits for nonacademic subjects, such as shop work, agriculture, music, industrial arts, homemaking, and commercial subjects.[3] The other fourteen state universities require either fifteen specific units in academic courses or do not list the nonacademic subjects among those acceptable for admission. The private universities ordinarily specify academic subjects as the only ones for which they will grant credit. The University of Illinois believes that high schools should offer courses in such fields as agriculture, art, commerce, home economics, industrial arts, and music and accepts them as a satisfactory preparation for college work. The University of Georgia expresses a similar belief. The Bulletin of the Virginia Polytechnical Institute declares that vocational agriculture serves fully as well in preparation for college, regardless of the curricula elected in college, as do the other high school courses, which are replaced by agriculture—that is, languages and sometimes a third year of mathematics or history. The Michigan Agreement[4] is of special interest.

[3] See Appendix 5, page 191.
[4] See Chapter IV, pages 67-68.

Another striking evidence of the possible close relationship of secondary vocational education and college entrance is offered by the principal of the San Jose (California) High School: "Three George F. Baker Scholarships are offered every year by Stanford University to competing graduates of California's trade and industrial vocational schools. A graduate of the machine shop in San Jose is one of the three ucky boys. To have such a school as Stanford recognize the poss. ility of finding ability and talent in schools such as ours is indeed encouraging. To offer a young man a six-thousand-dollar scholarship is a long step in the right direction. I believe that the Dean of the School of Education and his group should be highly commended for this practical evaluation of an educational program."

Benjamin Fine has reported that a survey by J. A. Yates on "the type of high-school curricula which has the best preparation for college" showed no significant difference in the value of any high-school curriculum over another for any particular curriculum or major in college. Although private institutions still require mostly the traditional academic subjects, we can see that progress has been made, even though the pace is slow.

Whatever further recognition there may be of the value of vocational subjects in preparing for study in college will undoubtedly be an inducement to secondary school administrators to organize vocational courses for those who are headed for college but find their special interests in vocations. Such liberalization of college entrance requirements should be encouraged in all institutions of higher education.

VALIDITY OF PRESENT COLLEGE ENTRANCE REQUIREMENTS

What is the validity of such present college entrance requirements as foreign languages, mathematics, and technical science? This study was not intended to provide and does not offer any answer to this question. It can touch upon it only tangentially.

The liberalization of college entrance requirements naturally means that if vocational subjects are accepted for college entrance, some other subjects must be omitted. Controversy usually rages around the foreign languages, mathematics, and technical science. Not only are they questioned as being valid for college entrance, but they are questioned as to their value as college subjects, and related to all of this is the question regarding the value of a college education itself. Of course, the answer lies in the aptitudes, interests, and abilities of the individual student. That means that the extent to which he can take "cultural" subjects depends upon the possibility of developing them out of and relating them to the student's basic interests. The only answer to this problem lies in intensive individual guidance and in flexible programming based upon the results of such guidance.

The solution is to give each individual boy or girl the opportunity to continue his or her education to the point where it begins to offer obviously and markedly diminishing returns. There are bound to be differences of opinion expressed by the student, the parent, the high school teacher, the college professor, and the general public that supports the school. However, with continued and intensified guidance, sooner or later concord of opinion results. In the meanwhile, insofar as the institutions of higher education can liberalize their entrance requirements and the secondary schools can intensify both their provisions for vocational education and their offerings of college entrance subjects (liberalized or not), the entire standard of education will be raised. In any case, it is imperative that school curricula should omit "useless" subjects dealing in inert ideas.

THE TECHNICAL INSTITUTE

For the last twenty years there has been much discussion about the technical institute and the junior college, and in certain areas, especially in New York State and California, much has been done in organizing these two-year, post-high school institutions. For the most part, they are terminal institutions where young people prepare for specific vocations. Admissions to these institutions should not depend on the offerings of "useless subjects" but should be wholly dependent upon the effectiveness of the student in his supposed special abilities.

THE FALLACY OF PUSHING UP THE AGE FOR VOCATIONAL EDUCATION

As previously pointed out,[5] probably the most effective type of procedure, in terms of child psychology, is that followed in the kindergarten. The youngsters are so young and so active that it is only through an appeal to interest and an offering of activity that they can be kept in order for any cooperative effort. However, from that point on there seems to be a gradual diminution of activity in favor of traditional educational and social demands— all this, despite the growing conviction that "there is no learning without interest" and that "we learn what we do." The place of vocational education and vocational education methodology is important to all ages. A *doing, youthful*, dynamic education, which is vocational education, is important at all times.

Recalling the quotations from Spears and Douglass,[6] it is important to note the tendency of academic educators to advocate the withholding of vocational education until the later high school years (eleventh and twelfth) or even till the post-high school years (thirteenth and fourteenth). Again, this study did not make any special examination of this particular problem. However, any casual consideration of the history of vocational education indicates that it was originally advocated because it was based on vital human interests and upon general acceptance of the belief that we "learn to do by doing." "Manual training" was a far cry

5 See Chapter V, page 74.
6 See Chapter IV, pages 61-64.

from vocational education, but, with all its limitations, it was soundly conceived. Vocational education was first given to delinquents because they *had* to be interested and they could learn *only* by doing. So the whole vocational educational movement was based on these theories, but now we see the tendency to forget them and to replace a psychological concept by a social one.

VOCATIONAL EDUCATION AND LIFE ADJUSTMENT

The appointment of the Life Adjustment Commission by the United States Office of Education has given impetus to the improvement of secondary education in terms of adjustment to the realities of life. The appointment was the result of the well-known Prosser Resolution. It was based upon the assumption that 20 percent of the population are being well prepared for college entrance, and that another 20 percent are being equally well prepared for the skilled occupations, but that the remaining 60 percent are not getting the type of education that definitely prepares them for anything.

The present study has been concerned with all three of these groups, but in various ways.

(1) Of the 20 percent of high school pupils who are successfully taught the skilled trades there are some who also desire and can profit by preparation for college entrance. They may wish both occupational and cultural education on the college level. This study indicates that a secondary program with these objectives is both desirable and feasible.

(2) Of the 20 percent of high school pupils preparing primarily for college entrance there may be an appreciable number who would want to prepare for a vocation. (In the Performing Arts Division of the Metropolitan Vocational High School a majority of the pupils, if given a choice between college entrance and preparation for drama, dance, or musical professions, would

choose the former. However, the opportunity to prepare for both college and an occupation is embraced with enthusiasm.) Again, this study confirms the possibility of serving this double purpose.

(3) Life adjustment for the 60 percent may consist of "better general education" (as many of the generalists say), or of preparation for skilled or semiskilled trades, or of a combination of both. Not having authentic data available, we can only offer again the suggestion that the more "doing," "activity," "work experience" (both in and out of school), the greater likelihood there is of effective education—even though the graduate does not later enter a trade for which he was trained.

Charles A. Prosser's whole life was devoted to vocational education and to the benefits that could arise from application of vocational contents and methods to education for *all* young people. Twenty-five years ago he was talking vehemently about thinking and intelligence as products of good methodology in vocational education. No doubt this was in his mind when he offered his famous Resolution. What else can any sound education be but life adjustment? So life adjustment education and Prosser's Resolution cannot be understood without understanding and implementing Prosser's sound, basic philosophy.

EDUCATION FOR FREE YOUTH

Life adjustment is education for free youth. There must be equality of opportunity. There must be free association, a common goal. People must work together. They must believe in each other's work because they are serving others and others are serving them. They must be common sharers in the task of making life livable. Vocational education assumes and works upon the principle that every individual is worthy of preparation for an occupation and every occupation is worthy of the individual who pursues it, whether it be manual, intellectual, or aesthetic, thus arriving at the "dignity of labor" by action rather than preachment. Whatever may be the dominant drive that impels one to seek an education, there is always the possibility of an approach on two fronts, the utilitarian and the cultural, or better, on one front that makes a culture of occupation and an occupation of culture. That it is desirable and feasible to organize a secondary school to serve such a purpose has been demonstrated in this study.

Most people would agree on how a mature adult should act in a scientific age, but they disagree upon the knowledge that should be put into his head and how it should be put there—in other words, about subject matter and methods in education. For centuries we took work as we found it. By learning what kind of work we like, pursuing and advancing in it intelligently, we may even beat the technological age. Obviously, "the good life" is neither mere drudgery nor all play, but a combination of both; so, preparation for the good life—education—must comprehend both. Since vocation is a part of living, vocational education can well be the integrating principle. And the integrating principle of vocation must necessarily be purpose, goal, end. Every boy or girl should be a young man or woman going somewhere. They should be free youth in the grip of rich and fruitful education.

Appendix 1

High Schools Surveyed

Paul Hayne Vocational H.S.	Birmingham, Alabama
Lanier H.S.	Montgomery, Alabama
Phoenix Technical H.S.	Phoenix, Arizona
Senior H.S.	Little Rock, Arkansas
Sacramento Senior H.S.	Sacramento, California
Gompers Trade School	San Francisco, California
San Jose H.S.	San Jose, California
Frank Wiggins Junior College	Los Angeles, California
East H.S.	Denver, Colorado
Hartford H.S.	Hartford, Connecticut
H. Fletcher Brown Vocational H. S.	Wilmington, Delaware
Anna Burdick Vocational H.S.	Washington, D.C.
Smith-Hughes Vocational H.S.	Atlanta, Georgia
Boise Senior H.S.	Boise, Idaho
Pocatello Senior H. S.	Pocatello, Idaho
Lane Technical H.S.	Chicago, Illinois
Peoria H.S.	Peoria, Illinois
Joliet Township H.S.	Joliet, Illinois
Gerstmeyer Technical H.S.	Terre Haute, Indiana
Washington H.S.	East Chicago, Indiana
Central H.S.	Fort Wayne, Indiana
Washington H. S.	Indianapolis, Indiana
Rosedale H.S.	Kansas City, Kansas
Lafayette H.S.	Lexington, Kentucky
Louisville Male H.S.	Louisville, Kentucky
Byrd H.S.	Shreveport, Louisiana

Portland H.S.	Portland, Maine
English H.S.	Boston, Massachusetts
Rindge Technical School	Cambridge, Massachusetts
Holyoke Trade School	Holyoke, Massachusetts
Holyoke H.S.	Holyoke, Massachusetts
South H.S.	Worcester, Massachusetts
Cass Technical H.S.	Detroit, Michigan
Senior H.S.	Rochester, Minnesota
Central H.S.	Jackson, Mississippi
Hadley Technical H.S.	St. Louis, Missouri
Senior H.S.	Springfield, Missouri
Butte H.S.	Butte, Montana
Reno H.S.	Reno, Nevada
Stevens H.S.	Claremont, New Hampshire
Albuquerque Senior H.S.	Albuquerque, New Mexico
Vocational Technical H.S.	Bayonne, New Jersey
Camden County Vocational H.S.	Merchantville, New Jersey
Essex County Vocational H.S.	Newark, New Jersey
Burgard Vocational H.S.	Buffalo, New York
Commerce H.S.	Yonkers, New York
Saunders Trade and Technical H.S.	Yonkers, New York
Metropolitan Vocational H.S.	New York, New York
Brooklyn H.S. of Automotive Trades	Brooklyn, New York
Brooklyn Technical H.S.	Brooklyn, New York
Boys H.S.	Brooklyn, New York
Alexander Hamilton Vocational H.S.	Brooklyn, New York
Midwood H.S.	Brooklyn, New York
Bronx H.S. of Science	New York, New York
H.S. of Music and Art	New York, New York
Stuyvesant H.S.	New York, New York
Christopher Columbus H.S.	New York, New York
Mont Pleasant H.S.	Schenectady, New York
Fargo Senior H.S.	Fargo, North Dakota
Hower Vocational H.S.	Akron, Ohio
East Liverpool H.S.	Oklahoma City, Oklahoma
Central H.S.	Oklahoma City, Oklahoma

Salem Senior H.S.	Salem, Oregon
McKeesport H.S.	McKeesport, Pennsylvania
Mt. Penn H.S.	Reading, Pennsylvania
Pottstown H.S.	Pottstown, Pennsylvania
Derry County Vocational H.S.	Hershey, Pennsylvania
Williamsport Senior H.S.	Williamsport, Pennsylvania
Rogers H.S.	Providence, Rhode Island
Spartanburg H.S.	Spartanburg, South Carolina
Central H.S.	Aberdeen, South Dakota
Central H.S.	Nashville, Tennessee
Crozier Technical H.S.	Dallas, Texas
San Antonio Vocational and Technical H.S.	San Antonio, Texas
South H.S.	Salt Lake City, Utah
John Marshall H.S.	Richmond, Virginia
Marysville H.S.	Marysville, Washington
Centralia H.S.	Centralia, Washington
R. A. Long H.S.	Longview, Washington
Walla Walla H.S.	Walla Walla, Washington
La Crosse Vocational and Adult Schools	LaCrosse, Wisconsin
Boys' Trade and Technical H.S.	Milwaukee, Wisconsin
East Fairmont H.S.	Fairmont, West Virginia

Material describing high-school courses was received also from Cincinnati, Cleveland, and Elyria, Ohio, and from the District of Columbia.

Appendix 2

Comparison of Semester Period Schedules in Industrial Arts and Vocational Courses

The data for the schools in the table below is representative of schedules in general and vocational high schools throughout the country. Comparison is made, in terms of semester periods, for Grades 10, 11, and 12, between the schedule in an industrial arts course in a New York City High School and the schedules in automobile mechanics courses in five vocational high schools. "Semester period" means the number of periods per week per semester.

COMPARATIVE SCHEDULES IN HIGH SCHOOLS BY SUBJECTS AND SEMESTER PERIODS

	Industrial Arts in N.Y.C. High School	Brooklyn H.S. for Auto Trades	Hadley Technical H.S. St. Louis	Camden County Vocational H.S.	Phoenix Technical H.S.	Burgard Vocational H.S. Buffalo
English	30	30	20	12	20	30
Social studies	25	15	20	12	20	10
Related drawing		7½	7	12	4[a]	
Physical education	30	15	4	24		12
Library			6	6		
Study or associated activity		20	10			
Applied science			15	12	10	20
Elective	30	15	5		10	10[b]
Applied mathematics			10	18		
Job relations			5			10
Business management		5			30[a]	
Nonsolids				2		
Accident prevention—first aid						
Hygiene	3	2½				
Music	2	2½				
Automotive theory		2½				
Diesel theory		2½				
Car-driving techniques		2½				
Shop	60	120	138	120	90[c]	120
Total	180[d]	240	240	218	180	212

[a] Physical education, ROTC, Drum and Bugle Corps.
[b] Trade drawing or advanced garage accounting.
[c] These 90 periods are approximately equal to shop time in other schools because shop meets for three hours each day as in the other schools, and would give a pupil two and one half more units (or twenty-five semester periods) than are required for graduation.
[d] One hundred eighty hours would represent a maximum load.

Appendix 3

College Preparatory Schedule of a General and Vocational School

The college preparatory course in a New York City general high school and the combined college preparatory and vocational course at Metropolitan Vocational High School, New York City, for grades 10, 11, and 12 are compared below in terms of semester periods.

	General High School	Metropolitan Vocational H.S.
English	30	30
Social studies	25	25
Science[a]		
Mathematics[a]	60–90	65
Foreign language[a]		
Physical education	30	12
Hygiene	3	5
Music	2	
Shop work		103
Total	150–180[b]	240

[a] Science, mathematics, and foreign languages are the three subjects in which pupils must complete a major sequence of three units (thirty semester hours) and two minor sequences of two units (twenty semester hours). Music and art are two other subjects which pupils in the general high school may present for minor sequences for the academic diploma.

[b] One hundred and eighty hours would represent a maximum load and would give a pupil two and one half more units than are required for graduation. Such a schedule may be taken only by those pupils who have an average of at least 75 per cent in each term. A total of 165 hours would be more representative.

Appendix 4

Analysis of Curricula and Requirements for Graduation from General High Schools

Curricula

1. Agriculture
2. Bookkeeping
3. Commercial
4. Cultural
5. Distributive education
6. Diversified occupations
7. Fine arts
8. General
9. Home economics
10. Latin-classical
11. Liberal
12. Manual arts
13. Music
14. Nurse's preparatory
15. Science
16. Stenographic
17. Technical
18. Vocational

Vocational Subjects Available

1. Agricultural
2. Auto mechanics
3. Aviation mechanics
4. Beauty culture
5. Building trades
6. Ceramics
7. Commercial
8. Commercial art
9. Cooperative
10. Crafts
11. Diversified occupations
12. Distributive occupations
13. Electric wiring
14. Homecrafts
15. Library training
16. Machine shop
17. Mechanical drawing
18. Metal
19. Printing
20. Radio
21. Woodworking

	Number of Units Required for Graduation	Number of Units Specified	Number of Units in Electives	Required Courses					Curricula	Shops and Vocational Courses Available
				English	Social Studies	Mathematics	Science	Physical Education		
Little Rock H. S., Little Rock, Arkansas	17½	9½	8	3	2	1 or 2	1 or 2	1½		7-8-11-12-13-16-17-19-21
Sidney Lanier H. S., Montgomery, Alabama										
General Course	17	9	8	4	1	1	2		2-3-5-6-8-9-10-12-15-16	
Manual Arts Course	17	13	4	4	1	3	2			
Latin Course	17	13	4	4	1	4				10

General Course pupils may substitute 2 units of language for science. Four units of Latin are required in Latin course, 3 Units of Shop in manual arts course.

	Number of Units Required for Graduation	Number of Units Specified	Number of Units in Electives	English	Social Studies	Mathematics	Science	Physical Education	Curricula	Shops and Vocational Courses Available
Sacramento Senior H. S., Sacramento, California	19½	8½	11	2½	1½	1	1	3		2-6-10-11-13-14-16-17-18-19-20-21

½ unit in orientation is required in all courses. Vocational courses are given on a one or two hour basis, generally for four terms. A grade of C in the one hour course is a pre-requisite for admission to one two hour course.

School										
East H. S. (grades 10-11-12), Denver, Colorado	15	4½	10½	1	1		1½		3-7-8-9-12-13	8-10-17-18-21

One unit in general education is required in all courses. Seniors may take vocational courses for three hours a day at the Denver Opportunity School.

Boise Senior H. S. (grades 10-11-12), Boise, Idaho	12½	4	8½	2½	1		½		5-6-7-13-15	2-17-19-21

Two of the 8½ units in electives must be in academic subjects.

Peoria H. S., Peoria, Illinois	16	9¼	6¾	3½	2	1	1	1	2-4-8-13-16-17-19	16-17-19

Additional unit requirements: art ⅛, music ⅛, home economics or industrial arts ½. Four units in the following vocational courses are available to pupils over sixteen years of age who have had three semesters of industrial arts: auto mechanics, building trades, machine shop, radio and electronics, commercial art, beauty culture.

Joliet Township H. S., Joliet, Illinois	18	10	8	3	3	1	2		1-3-8-9-18	2-13-16-17-18-19-21

Additional unit requirement: general shop or home economics. The ten units required of all pupils are designated as "General Education" courses.

Central H. S., Fort Wayne, Indiana	16	9	7	3	2	1	1	1	3-8-12-17-18	2-16-17-21

Additional unit requirement: health and safety. Vocational courses provide one period of shop in grades 9 and 10, and 3 hours of shop in Grades 11 and 12.

Portland H. S., Portland, Maine	16	5	11	4	1				3-7-8-9-12-15	2-13-16-17-19-21

Choice of electives varies with curriculum. Shop courses are given for ten periods per week in grades 10-11-12. Pupils carry three or four academic subjects in addition to the shop work.

Analysis of Curricula and Requirements for Graduation from General High Schools—Cont.

	Number of Units Required for Graduation	Number of Units Specified	Number of Units in Electives	Required Courses					Curricula	Shops and Vocational Courses Available
				English	Social Studies	Mathematics	Science	Physical Education		
Holyoke, H. S., Holyoke, Mass.	16 (In Majors)	7	9	4	1	1	1		1-3-5-8-14-18	
Rochester Senior H. S. (grades 10-11-12), Rochester, Minnesota	12	5	7	3	2	1	1	3 years required	1-3-18	1-2-19-21
Senior High School (grades 10-11-12), Springfield, Missouri	13	9	4	2	3		2	1	1-2-3-5-6-8-9-12-13-16-18	1-2-3-5-8-10-11-13-14-17-18-19-20-21-16
Butte H. S., Butte, Montana	16	4½	11½	3	1½			2 years required	3-8-9-10-12-15	2-16-17-21

Holyoke, H. S., Holyoke, Mass. School provides a special two year general vocational course for girls. Trade training is presented in cooperation with Holyoke Trade School beginning with tenth grade; pupils take two periods or the high school (English 3 years, algebra, geometry, and American history) plus shop at the Trade School. The regular high school diploma will be awarded upon completion of the course plus a trade school certificate. Shop or home economics are required in the 9th year.

Senior High School (grades 10-11-12), Springfield, Missouri. Additional unit requirement: handwork. School offers program in general education. This is a comprehensive high school. Shops are offered for 2 semesters only. Shops on vocational basis meet for three hours.

Butte H. S., Butte, Montana. Only one year's work in each shop is offered. (Four years of Manual Arts constitute a major and include one year in each of the following: woodwork, machine shop, mechanical drawing, and auto mechanics.) Machine shop and auto mechanics may be elected by juniors and seniors only.

School										
Albuquerque H. S., Albuquerque, New Mexico	16	7½	8½	3	2	1	1	½	3-9-12	1-2-3-16-17-18-19-21

Vocational course majors may elect 8 units in vocational work.

| Fargo Senior H. S. (grades 10-11-12), Fargo, North Dakota | 12 | 4 | 8 | 2 | 2 | | | | 3-9-10-12-15-16 | 17-18-19-21 |

All curricula require minimum of ten academic units. Shops may be taken for four terms for five periods per week.

| Central H. S. (grades 10-11-12), Oklahoma City, Okla. | 12½ | 6 | 6½ | 3 | 1 | 1 | ½ | | 3-5-6-8-9-12-18 | 2-3-11-13-16-17-18-19-20 |

Auto mechanics, printing, and sheet metal are carried on a vocational basis with 2 or 3 units of credit for a year.

| Salem Senior H. S. (grades 10-11-12), Salem, Oregon | 15 | 9 | 6 | 3 | 2 | 1 | 3 | | 1-2-3-5-6-8-9-12 | 1-2-10-15-17-18-19-21 |

| Pottstown H. S. (grades 10-11-12), Pottstown, Penna. | 12 | 5 | 7 | 3 | 2 | | | | 3-4-8-9-10-12-15-18 | 13-16-17-19-21 |

Choice of electives depends upon curriculum. Shop work is on a vocational basis for the three years. Vocational course requires: English, 3 years; vocational math, 2 years; U. S. history, 1 year; drawing, 1 year; science, 2 years. "Subjects in the boys' vocational department are below college accrediting standards and cannot be used for college entrance."

| Spartanburg H. S., Spartanburg, S. C. | 16 | 6 | 10 | 4 | 2 | | | | 5-6-8-9-12-15 | 2-16-20 |

Choice of electives depends upon curriculum. Shop work on a vocational basis may be taken in 11th and 12th year.

Appendix 5

Vocational Credits Accepted for State University Admission

Alabama	4	Montana	*b*
Arizona*a*	5–6	Nebraska	*b*
Arkansas	4–6	Nevada	5
California	0	New Hampshire*a*	3
Colorado*	3	New Jersey (Rutgers)	0
Connecticut	3–4	New Mexico*a*	4
Delaware	3	North Carolina	4
Florida	*b*	North Dakota*a*	4
Georgia*a*	3	Ohio	0–5
Idaho	4–6	Oklahoma	*b*
Illinois*a*	2	Oregon	*b*
	(as industrial arts)	Penn State	0
Indiana	*b*	Rhode Island	0
Iowa	*b*	South Carolina*a*	3–½
Kansas*a*	*b*	South Dakota*a*	5
Kentucky	*b*	Tennessee	2–4
Louisiana*a*	3	Texas	2–4
Maine	*b*	Utah	2–½–3
Michigan	5	Vermont	0
Minnesota	3–5	Virginia	4
Mississippi	3	Washington	5–7
Missouri*a*	4	West Virginia	4

a These universities will accept in the elective category any courses which are accepted by an accredited high school for its diploma.

b These universities do not specifically mention the number of units in vocational courses which are acceptable.

Appendix 6

Some Typical High School Programs

Gerstmeyer Technical High School, Terre Haute, Indiana

First Semester	No. of Credits	Second Semester	No. of Credits
	First Year		
English I	1	English II	1
Guidance	1	Health and safety	1
General mathematics	1	General mathematics	1
General shop	1	General shop	1
Physical education	2/10	Physical education	3/10
	Second Year		
English III	1	English IV	1
American history	1	American history II	1
Biology I	1	Biology II	1
General shop	1	General shop	1
Physical education	2/10	Physical education	3/10
	Third Year		
English V	1	English VI	1
Related	1	Related	1
Trade subjects	2	Trade subjects	2
	Fourth Year		
Related	1	Related	1
Trade subjects	2	Trade subjects	2
U.S. Government	1		

Derry Township Vocational High School, Hershey, Pennsylvania

	Periods per Week	Number of Weeks	Credit
Tenth Grade			
English	7	19	1
American and Industrial History	7	19	1
Related Shop Mathematics	7	19	1
Related Drawing I	5	19	½
Health	2	19	⅓
Physical Education	2	19	⅓
Shop	30	19	2
Eleventh Grade			
English	7	19	1
Industrial Economics	4	19	½
Related Geometry or Shop Mathematics	4	19	½
Related Chemistry	8	19	1
Related Drawing II	4	19	¼
Physical Education	2	19	⅓
Study	1	19	0
Shop	30	19	2
Twelfth Grade			
English	7	19	1
Problems of Democracy	4	19	½
Related Trigonometry or shop mathematics	4	19	½
Related Physics	8	19	1
Related Drawing III	4	19	1
Physical Education	2	19	⅓
Study	1	19	0
Shop	30	19	2
		Total	17

Hadley Technical High School, St. Louis, Missouri
Auto Mechanics (Boys)

First Semester	Periods per Week	Credits per Term	Second Semester	Periods per Week	Credits per Term
		Tenth	Grade		
English 2	5	1	English 4	5	1
World history	5	1	World history	5	1
General industrial			Auto mechanics shop	20	2
shop (metal,			Applied science	5	1
wood, electric)	20	2	Physical education	2	¼
Related drawing	7	1	Study of assigned		
Physical education	2	¼	activities	2	0
Library	1	0	Library	1	0
	40	5¼		40	5¼
		Eleventh	Grade		
English 5	5	1	English 6	5	1
U.S. History	5	1	U.S. History	5	1
Auto mechanics			Auto mechanics		
shop 2	20	2	shop 3	20	2
Applied science 2	5	1	Applied science 3	5	1
Study and/or assigned			Study and/or assigned		
activities	4	¼	activities	4	¼
Library	1	0	Library	1	0
	40	5–5¼		40	5–5¼
		Twelfth	Grade		
Auto mechanics			Auto mechanics		
shop 4	20	2	shop 5	20	2
Welding (arc)	9	1	Welding (gas)	9	1
Applied mathe-			Applied mathe-		
matics 1	5	1	matics	5	1
Elective	5	½–1	Job relations	5	1
Library	1	0	Library	1	0
	40	4½–5		40	5

Appendix 6

Recommended Electives

American problems 1, 2	5	1
Radio workshop	5	1
Creative writing	5	1
Senior science 1, 2	7	1
Typewriting 1, 2	5	½

The Relationship Between the Basic Vocational-Technical Course and the Vocational-Technical Course in the Williamsport Senior High School, Williamsport, Pennsylvania, Based on a Thirty-Eight-Week Student Year, Thirty Clock Hours per Week

	Basic Vocational			Vocational-Technical		
	Clock Hours per Week by School Year					
	10	11	12	10	11	12
Shop	15	15	15	15	15	15
Related math	5	3	3	5	6	6
English	2¼	2½	2½	2¼	3¼	3¼
Social studies	2¼	2¼	2¼	2¼	3¼	3¼
Related science	2¼	3¾	3¾	2¼	3¼	3¼
Related drafting	1¼	2¼	2¼	1¼	1¼	1¼
Physical education	2	1¼	1¼	2	2	2

NOTE: In the case of vocational-technical pupils, related science and mathematics consist in part of sufficient algebra, trigonometry, geometry, physics, and chemistry to meet the college career planned by the individual.

Appendix 6

Cass Technical High School, Detroit, Michigan
Automotive Curriculum

First Semester	Periods per Week	Credits per Term	Second Semester	Periods per Week	Credits per Term
		Tenth	Grade		
English 3	5	5	English 4	5	5
Mathematics 3 (alg.)	5	5	Mathematics 4 (plane geometry)	5	5
Automotive Mechanics 1	10	5	Automotive mech. 2	10	5
Mechanical drawing 3	5	2½	Mechanical draw. 4	5	2½
Health Education 3	5	2½	Health Education 4	5	2½
			Chemistry 1	7	5
	30	20		37	25
		Eleventh	Grade		
English 5	5	5	English 6	5	5
Mathematics 5 (plane geometry)	5	5	Mathematics 6 (trigonometry)	5	5
Automotive Mechanics 3	10	5	Auto mechanics 4	10	5
Chemistry 2	7	5	Physics 1	7	5
Mechanical drawing	5	2½	American history 1	5	5
	32	22½		37	25
		Twelfth	Grade		
Mathematics 7 (solid geometry)	5	5	English 8	5	5
Automotive Mechanics 5	10	5	Auto Mechanics 6	10	5
American history 2	5	5	Civics	5	5
Physics 2	7	5	Metallurgy 1	7	5
Electives[a]	10	5			
	37	25		27	20

[a] Electives: mechanical drafting 6, advanced machine shop, college algebra, radio construction, or advanced garage practice. Certain other substitutions may be made if approved by the curriculum head and the principal.

Bibliography

ANDERSON, L. F., *History of Manual and Industrial School Education*, New York, D. Appleton & Company, 1926.

BENNETT, CHARLES A., *History of Manual and Industrial Education up to 1917*, Peoria, Manual Arts Press, 1926.

BRUBACHER, JOHN S., *A History of the Problems of Education*, New York, McGraw-Hill Book Company, 1947.

CAREY, EVERETT, and others, *General Education in the American High School*, Chicago, Scott, Foresman & Company, 1942.

CASWELL, HOLLIS L., COREY, STEPHEN M., and others, *The American High School: Its Responsibility and Opportunity*, Eighth Yearbook of the John Dewey Society, New York, Harper & Brothers, 1946.

CASWELL, HOLLIS L., and associates, *Curriculum Improvement*, New York, Bureau of Publications, Teachers College, Columbia University, 1950.

COOLEY, EDWIN G., *The Need for Vocational Schools in the United States*, Chicago, Commercial Club for Chicago, 1914.

DOUGLASS, HARL R., *The High School Curriculum*, The Ronald Press Company, New York, 1947.

Education for All American Youth, Washington, The Educational Policies Commission, National Education Association of the United States and the American Association of School Administrators, 1944.

EDWARDS, NORTON, and RICHEY, HERMAN G., *The School in the American Social Order*, Boston, Houghton Mifflin Company, 1947.

FINE, BENJAMIN, *Admission to American Colleges*, New York, Harper & Brothers, 1946.

FRENCH, HULL, and DODDS, *American High School Administration*, New York, Rinehart & Company, 1951.

GILES, McCUTCHEON, and ZECHIEL, *Exploring the Curriculum*, New York, Harper & Brothers, 1942.

HIBBERT, FRANCIS AIDAN, *The Influence and Development of English Guilds*, London, Cambridge University Press, 1891.

Higher Education for American Democracy, Vol. I., Establishing the Goals, A report of the President's Commission on Higher Education, Washington, U.S. Government Printing Office, 1947.

HOLT, WILLIAM STULL, *The Federal Board for Vocational Education*, New York, D. Appleton & Company, 1922.

HULL, J. DAN, *A Primer of Life Adjustment Education for Youth*, Chicago, American Technical Society, 1949.

JONES, GALEN, "High School of the Future," *Teachers College Record*, April, 1949.

KAHLER, ALFRED, and HAMBURGER, ERNEST, *Education for an Industrial Age,* Ithaca, Cornell University Press, 1948.

KALLEN, HORACE M., *The Education of Free Men*, New York, Farrar, Straus & Company, 1949.

KELLER, FRANKLIN J., *Principles of Vocational Education*, Boston, D. C. Heath & Company, 1948.

KRUGMAN, MORRIS, and WILSON, FRANCES, *Studies of Student Personnel*, The New York City Study of Vocational Education, Albany, University of the State of New York, January, 1951.

MARITAIN, JACQUES, *Education at the Crossroads*, New Haven, Yale University Press, 1943.

Planning for American Youth, Washington, Bulletin of the National Association of Secondary School Principals, 1944.

Planning Education for American Youth, Washington, Bulletin of the National Association of Secondary School Principals, 1949.

PARKES, GEORGE H., *A High School Technical-Vocational Curriculum*, Washington, Bulletin of the National Association of Secondary School Principals, May, 1950.

QUIGLEY, THOMAS H., *In The Sweat of Thy Face*, Atlanta, T. E. Smith & Company, 1942.

PROSSER, C. A., and QUIGLEY, THOMAS H., *Vocational Education in a Democracy*, Chicago, American Technical Society, 1949.

RENARD, GEORGE, *Guilds in the Middle Ages*, London, G. Bell & Sons, Ltd., 1919.

SEARS, WILLIAM PAUL, *Roots of Vocational Education*, New York, J. Wiley & Sons, 1931.

SPEARS, HAROLD, *The Emerging High School Curriculum and Its Direction*, New York, American Book Company, 1940.

TEAD, ORDWAY, "Major Issues in Today's Higher Education," *College and University*, July, 1949.

Vocational Education in the New York City High Schools, Albany, University of the State of New York, 1951.

WASKIN, LEON S., *Michigan Secondary School-College Agreement*, Bulletin of the National Association of Secondary School Principals, Washington, January, 1949.

WHITEHEAD, ALFRED NORTH, *The Aims of Education and Other Essays*, New York, The Macmillan Company, 1929.

WILBER, GORDON O., *Industrial Arts in General Education*, Scranton, Educational Text Book Company, 1948.

Index

Set in Linotype Times Roman
Format by Edwin H. Kaplin
Manufactured by The Haddon Craftsmen, Inc.
Published by HARPER & BROTHERS, *New York*